# BORN AGAIN TO ENTER INTO JESUS' KINGDOM

# BORN AGAIN TO ENTER INTO JESUS' KINGDOM:

## RECEIVING GOD THE FATHER'S SPIRITUAL DNA

*Kathy,*

*You are a blessing !*

## DR. DAVID M. SUMMERS

*Love in Christ,*

*David M. Summers*

Lamb's Book Publishing

Born Again To Enter Into Jesus' Kingdom: Receiving God the Father's Spiritual DNA

Lamb's Book Publishing

For additional copies of this book, visit spiritualdnabook.com

Printed in the United States of America

ISBN: 979-8-218-05635-3

All scripture quotations are taken from the King James Version of the Bible (emphasis added).

To my wife, Lorna Rose Summers,
and to my daughter, Noah Elisabeth Summers,
without whom I would not be spiritually at the place
the Holy Spirit has me.


With gratitude to my son,
Samuel Elisha Summers and his family,
for their love and support.

# ACKNOWLEDGEMENTS

Thank you Holy Spirit for this, your book. It is a blessing that you have discipled me starting as a babe in Christ.

Many men and women of God have sowed into my spiritual life as well. This book is part of their harvest. To God be the glory.

Thank you to simplythebible, my editor, for helping to make this book the best it could be.

Thank you to Rose Harris (RoseHarrisDesign.com) for producing the cover of the book.

# INTRODUCTION

Born Again To Enter Into Jesus' Kingdom will explain how you can be supernaturally born again and go to Heaven instead of Hell after your death. You will learn how to become a son or daughter of God the Father - having His spiritual DNA. Want your Christian life to be supernatural? Don't want to sin but keep struggling?

Find out how your sinful nature can be destroyed.

Learn how to emerge fully from the Spiritual Birth Canal.

Understand how easy it is to walk in the Holy Spirit.

Comprehend the Gospel of Jesus Christ fully.

Be able to present the Gospel to others so that they can believe in God, repent of their sins, and become born again.

Discover the difference between Old Covenant saints and New Covenant saints.

Live spiritually with resurrection power.

This book will help you become a part of the spotless bride of Christ who is being prepared for a great wedding.

Do you desire freedom instead of fear? This book is for you.

# CONTENTS

# YOU MUST BE BORN AGAIN

How do we get into God's eternal Kingdom? How do we not go to Hell, the Lake of Fire (Rev. 20:15), God's place of eternal punishment for sin? Is there a definitive answer to these important questions?

Yes, there is!

Jesus said that in order to enter into His Kingdom, you must be born again.

## John 3:3 (KJV)

[3] Jesus answered and said unto him, Verily, verily, I say unto thee, <u>Except a man be born again</u>, he cannot see the kingdom of God.

## John 3:5 (KJV)

[5] Jesus answered, Verily, verily, I say unto thee, <u>Except a man be born of water and *of* the Spirit, he cannot enter into the kingdom of God.</u>

There is the natural realm, and there is the supernatural realm; the physical which we can see, and the spiritual which is invisible. When Jesus said to Nicodemus, a ruler of the Jewish people, that he had to be born again to get into the Kingdom of God, Nicodemus naturally thought Jesus was talking about the physical world.

## John 3:4 (KJV)

[4] Nicodemus saith unto him, How can a man be born when he is old? <u>can he enter the second time into his mother's womb, and be born?</u>

Jesus made the distinction between physical birth and spiritual birth.

## John 3:6 (KJV)
⁶ That which is <u>born of the flesh is flesh</u>; and that which is <u>born of the Spirit is spirit</u>.

## John 1:12-13 (KJV)
¹² But as many as received him, to them gave he power <u>to become the sons of God</u>, *even* to them that believe on his name:
¹³ <u>Which were born</u>, not of blood, nor of the will of the flesh, nor of the will of man, but <u>of God</u>.

Jesus explained that He was talking about spiritual birth, not physical birth. When we are born into this physical world, we have physical DNA (DeoxyriboNucleic Acid) from our physical parents, our biological father and mother, but we also have spiritual DNA from our spiritual father, Satan, because our sin natures are from him. Human DNA is the foundational basis that determines a person's physical body. Human spiritual DNA is the foundational basis that determines a person's spiritual body of sin, the sin nature. When we are born, we are all sinners with satanic spiritual DNA and are all children of wrath, that is, heading toward the Lake of Fire, the just and final eternal place of punishment for the wicked.

## Romans 6:6 (KJV)
⁶ Knowing this, that our old man is crucified with *him*, that <u>the body of sin</u> might be destroyed, that henceforth we should not serve sin.

## Matthew 25:31-33 (KJV)
³¹ When the <u>Son of man shall come in his glory</u>, and all the holy angels with him, <u>then shall he sit upon the throne of his glory</u>:
³² And <u>before him shall be gathered all nations</u>: and he shall

separate them one from another, as a shepherd divideth *his* sheep from the goats:

<sup>33</sup> And <u>he shall set the sheep on his right hand, but the goats on the left</u>.

## Matthew 25:41 (KJV)

<sup>41</sup> Then shall <u>he say also unto them on the left hand</u>, <u>Depart from me, ye cursed, into everlasting fire</u>, prepared for the devil and his angels:

## Matthew 25:46 (KJV)

<sup>46</sup> And <u>these shall go away into everlasting punishment</u>: <u>but the righteous into life eternal</u>.

**We are created with physical and spiritual DNA at conception. At our births, we are therefore born both physically and spiritually which is why Jesus speaks of being born again.**

## Psalm 51:5 (KJV)

<sup>5</sup> Behold, I was shapen in iniquity; and <u>in sin did my mother conceive me</u>.

## John 8:38-44 (KJV)

<sup>38</sup> I speak that which I have seen with <u>my Father</u>: and ye do that which ye have seen with <u>your father</u>.

<sup>39</sup> They answered and said unto him, Abraham is our father. Jesus saith unto them, If ye were Abraham's children, ye would do the works of Abraham.

<sup>40</sup> But now <u>ye seek to kill me</u>, a man that hath told you the truth, which I have heard of God: this did not Abraham.

<sup>41</sup> <u>Ye do the deeds of your father</u>. Then said they to him, We be not born of fornication; we have one Father, *even* God.

<sup>42</sup> Jesus said unto them, If God were your Father, ye would love me: for <u>I proceeded forth and came from God</u>; neither came I of myself, but he sent me.

[43] Why do ye not understand my speech? *even* because ye cannot hear my word.
[44] Ye are of *your* father the devil, and the lusts of your father ye will do. He was a murderer from the beginning, and abode not in the truth, because there is no truth in him. When he speaketh a lie, he speaketh of his own: for he is a liar, and the father of it.

Jesus revealed that those to whom He was speaking were all born with Satan's spiritual DNA, and thus Satan was their spiritual father. However, Jesus was born having God the Father's spiritual DNA, that is, He was born in the flesh but without a sinful nature and had the Holy Spirit indwelling Him spiritually.

Jesus is both the Son of Man and the Son of God. Jesus was born physically in the flesh with the seed (DNA) of both Abraham and King David, His ancestral physical fathers, making Him the Son of Man. Spiritually, Jesus was born in the Spirit with the seed (DNA) of God, His spiritual Father, making Him the Son of God.

## Hebrews 2:16 (KJV)

[16] For verily he took not on *him the nature of* angels; but he took on *him* the seed of Abraham.

## Galatians 3:16 (KJV)

[16] Now to Abraham and his seed were the promises made. He saith not, And to seeds, as of many; but as of one, And to thy seed, which is Christ.

## Romans 1:3-4 (KJV)

[3] Concerning his Son Jesus Christ our Lord, which was made of the seed of David according to the flesh;
[4] And declared *to be* the Son of God with power, according to the spirit of holiness, by the resurrection from the dead:

## 1 John 3:9 (KJV)

[9] Whosoever is born of God doth not commit sin; for his seed remaineth in him: and he cannot sin, because he is born of God.

## 2 Corinthians 5:19 (KJV)

[19] To wit, that God was in Christ, reconciling the world unto himself, not imputing their trespasses unto them; and hath committed unto us the word of reconciliation.

Jesus revealed that through belief in Him (being born again) our spiritual DNA could be changed from Satan's to God's and, thus, we may escape condemnation.

## John 3:15-18 (KJV)

[15] That whosoever believeth in him [Jesus] should not perish, but have eternal life.
[16] For God so loved the world, that he gave his only begotten Son, that whosoever believeth in him should not perish, but have everlasting life.
[17] For God sent not his Son into the world to condemn the world; but that the world through him might be saved.
[18] He that believeth on him is not condemned: but he that believeth not is condemned already, because he hath not believed in the name of the only begotten Son of God.

## John 3:36 (KJV)

[36] He that believeth on the Son hath everlasting life: and he that believeth not the Son shall not see life; but the wrath of God abideth on him.

We are all made in the flesh (physical) with sinful natures (spiritual), that is, having the spiritual DNA of Satan who, in this sense, is our spiritual father. Because we are born spiritually as sinners, we are all doomed to eternal punishment, and the wrath of God is already upon us.

Jesus was made in the likeness of sinful flesh but without the sinful nature.

## Romans 8:3 (KJV)

³ For what the law could not do, in that it was weak through the flesh, <u>God sending his own Son in the likeness of sinful flesh</u>, and for sin, <u>condemned sin in the flesh</u>:

## 2 Corinthians 5:21 (KJV)

²¹ For he hath made him *to be* sin for us, <u>who knew no sin</u>; that we might be made the righteousness of God in him.

## Hebrews 4:15 (KJV)

¹⁵ For we have not an high priest which cannot be touched with the feeling of our infirmities; but was in all points tempted like as *we are, yet* <u>without sin</u>.

Jesus was just like us in that He was made flesh, but His spiritual DNA was that of the Son of God, and when He was tempted to sin, being without the sin nature, He was free from sin and could choose perfectly not to sin. He was a man who lived His whole life obeying God, <u>always choosing</u> not to sin, <u>and so He condemned sin in the flesh</u>.

We, on the other hand, have satanic spiritual DNA as the foundation of our spiritual life when we are born, and we are not free from sin but are rather the servants of sin, and, consequently, choose to sin when tempted. Outwardly, even when it appears that we do righteously, our righteousness is foundationally apart from God and is not righteous.

## John 8:34 (KJV)

³⁴ Jesus answered them, Verily, verily, I say unto you, <u>Whosoever committeth sin is the servant of sin</u>.

## Romans 6:20 (KJV)

[20] For when ye were the servants of sin, ye were free from righteousness.

## Isaiah 64:6 (KJV)

[6] But we are all as an unclean *thing*, and all our righteousnesses *are* as filthy rags; and we all do fade as a leaf; and our iniquities, like the wind, have taken us away.

## Matthew 23:28 (KJV)

[28] Even so ye also outwardly appear righteous unto men, but within ye are full of hypocrisy and iniquity.

## Romans 3:10 (KJV)

[10] As it is written, There is none righteous, no, not one:

How is it that we are all born with the spiritual DNA of Satan?

In the Garden of Eden, it biblically appears that Adam and Eve started by being spiritual DNA neutral, not having God the Father's or Satan's spiritual DNA. If they were created spiritually with the indwelling Holy Spirit, then Adam and Eve would have been created similar to Jesus who never sinned in the flesh. But we know, they did sin.

God created Adam and Eve in His own image (Gen. 1:27), and everything God created, including Adam and Eve, was not only good, but very good (Gen 1:31). Adam and Eve were not created with evil spirits in them, in the spiritual realm, but they did not have the Holy Spirit dwelling within them in the spiritual realm. In the spiritual realm, they only had their individual spirits and were otherwise spiritually DNA neutral. The LORD God was with them in the Garden of Eden, walking with them (Genesis 3:8) but was not within them spiritually.

Adam and Eve were also without consciences, the inner sense of right and wrong, because before eating from the tree of the <u>knowledge</u> of good and evil, <u>they did not know</u> about evil. In the physical realm, Adam and Eve <u>only knew good</u>, since they existed in what God had created which was all good.

However, having free will to choose, when Adam and Eve chose to disobey the LORD God, having listened to Satan, having not believed the LORD God (Genesis 2:17 "…for in the day that thou eatest thereof thou shalt surely die."), having not had faith, they got the spiritual DNA <u>of Satan</u>. They were henceforth sinners, having sin natures. They received <u>evil consciences</u>. From then on, they knew good and evil, and since they had received their consciences by sinning, their consciences were evil. Everyone born since then (except Jesus) has been born with a sinful nature and an evil conscience.

When Adam and Eve chose not to believe the LORD God and to reject His Word, the consequence was spiritual death. When they ate the fruit, they died spiritually as God had said they would. In addition to spiritual death, the consequence of Adam's sin was physical death entering the world.

## Romans 5:19 (KJV)

[19] For as <u>by one man's</u> [Adam's] <u>disobedience many were made sinners</u>, so by the obedience of one [Jesus] shall many be made righteous.

## Romans 5:12 (KJV)

[12] Wherefore, <u>as by one man</u> [Adam] <u>sin [sin natures] entered into the world</u>, <u>and death by sin</u>; and so <u>death passed upon all men</u>, <u>for that all have sinned</u>:

Cain, Adam and Eve's first child, had the spiritual DNA of Satan, his spiritual father.

## 1 John 3:12 (KJV)

[12] Not as <u>Cain</u>, *who* <u>was of that wicked one</u>, and slew his brother. And wherefore slew he him? Because his own works were evil, and his brother's righteous.

By being born again, we receive the Holy Spirit, which is the spiritual DNA of God, our new spiritual Father; by his blood, Jesus purges our <u>evil</u> consciences and makes them into <u>good</u> consciences.

## Hebrews 9:14 (KJV)

[14] How much more shall <u>the blood of Christ</u>, who through the eternal Spirit offered himself without spot to God, <u>purge your conscience</u> from dead works to serve the living God?

## Hebrews 10:22 (KJV)

[22] Let us draw near with a true heart in full assurance of faith, having our hearts sprinkled from an <u>evil conscience</u>, and our bodies washed with pure water.

## 1 Timothy 1:19 (KJV)

[19] Holding faith, and a <u>good conscience</u>; which some having put away concerning faith have made shipwreck:

What makes up spiritual DNA? Let us first consider physical DNA. We understand that children inherit it from their biological mothers and fathers. Consequently, children will talk, behave and look similar to one or both of their parents, since the children have inherited certain traits which manifest in the physical realm.

So what makes up spiritual DNA, the sin nature which impels us to sin? Since we are talking about the invisible spiritual realm, we understand that spirits are in the spiritual realm. Evil spirits are spiritual beings like demons who do not have physical bodies but do have names and personalities such as "legion" (Luke 8:30) and "jealousy" (Numbers 5:14). Evil spirits want to reside in human bodies because they need physical bodies to manifest. For example, a lying spirit needs a mouth and tongue to lie.

Conceptualizing the sin nature as the spiritual DNA of Satan and as evil spirits helps to explain how the LORD has the "iniquities of the fathers visit upon the children unto the third and fourth generations" (Exodus 20:5, Exodus 34:7, & Numbers 14:18). It is well observed that certain families manifest one or more repeating sins, such as adultery, murder, suicide, and alcoholism, in successive generations. Thus, the grandfather committing adultery, the father committing adultery, and the son committing adultery are all examples of the spirit of adultery being passed down in the satanic spiritual DNA of parents to their children. A person may spiritually possess, but not physically manifest, an inherited generational evil spirit, for example, the spirit of adultery, by being tempted to commit adultery, but choosing not to do so. An evil spirit of adultery will compel the person to sin, but a person must choose to sin. For example, Cain had the evil spirit of murder from his spiritual DNA father, Satan, and was tempted to murder Abel and chose to do so.

We understand that children (and adults) inherit in the spiritual realm their sin natures, the spiritual DNA from their biological mothers and fathers. Consequently, children and adults will spiritually often be observed to talk, behave and look similar to one or both of their parents.

In contrast to the <u>many</u> evil spirits which compose satanic spiritual DNA, there is <u>only one</u> Spirit who makes up God the Father's spiritual DNA, and that is the Holy Spirit. Holy Spirit is God and is the seed of God the Father in us spiritually.

## 1 Corinthians 6:17 (KJV)

[17] But he that is joined unto the Lord is <u>one spirit</u>.

## 1 Corinthians 12:13 (KJV)

[13] For by <u>one Spirit</u> are we all baptized into one body, whether *we be* Jews or Gentiles, whether *we be* bond or free; and have been all made to drink into <u>one Spirit</u>.

## Ephesians 2:18 (KJV)

[18] For through him we both have access by <u>one Spirit</u> unto the Father.

## Ephesians 4:4 (KJV)

[4] *There is* one body, and <u>one Spirit</u>, even as ye are called in one hope of your calling;

## 1 John 3:9 (KJV)

[9] Whosoever is <u>born of God</u> doth not commit sin; for <u>his seed</u> remaineth in him: and he cannot sin, because he is born of God.

We must be born again as children of God to have new spiritual lives, to have the spiritual DNA of God the Father, to be with God for all eternity in His Home (John 14:2). God the Father created man in His own image (Genesis 1:27) in order to have a family. As children of God, we all have direct personal relationships with God: Father, Jesus, and Holy Spirit. True Christianity is about relationship, not about religion, and about whom we know, not about what we know. Christianity is about our spiritual identity, who we are, that is, who is our spiritual DNA Father.

In the physical realm, a <u>paternity test</u> is done to determine if a man is a child's biological father. In the spiritual realm, finding the presence of the Holy Spirit, God the Father's spiritual DNA, within a person is the <u>paternity test</u> which determines that God the Father is the person's spiritual father.

## Romans 8:9 (KJV)

[9] But ye are not in the flesh, but in the Spirit, <u>if so be that the Spirit of God dwell in you</u>. Now <u>if any man have not the Spirit of Christ</u>, <u>he is none of his</u>.

The most important thing to do in our lives is to be born again into Jesus' Kingdom. When we have been born again, we have sought the Kingdom of God <u>first</u>.

## Matthew 6:33 (KJV)

[33] But <u>seek ye first the kingdom of God, and his righteousness</u>; and all these things shall be added unto you.

Now let us look at how Jesus made a way for us to have new spiritual DNA lives whose spiritual Father is God.

# OUR SATANIC SPIRITUAL LIFE CRUCIFIED

Jesus provides sinners a great salvation, for He is God the Father's offering for our sins. Jesus lived a complete life of obedience to God the Father who put our iniquities upon Jesus. Jesus chose to die in our place and to shed His precious blood for our sins. Jesus defeated death by being raised from the dead, and by His resurrection was declared to be the Son of God who can give us Eternal Life.

## Hebrews 2:3 (KJV)
³ How shall we escape, if we neglect so <u>great salvation</u>; which at the first began to be spoken by the Lord, and was confirmed unto us by them that heard *him*;

## Isaiah 53:10-11 (KJV)
¹⁰ Yet it pleased <u>the LORD</u> to bruise him; he hath put *him* to grief: when <u>thou shalt make his soul an offering for sin</u>, he shall see *his* seed, he shall prolong *his* days, and the pleasure of the LORD shall prosper in his hand.
¹¹ <u>He shall see of the travail of his soul</u>, *and* <u>shall be satisfied</u>: by his knowledge shall <u>my righteous servant justify many; for he shall bear their iniquities</u>.

## Isaiah 53:6 (KJV)
⁶ All we like sheep have gone astray; we have turned every one to his own way; and <u>the LORD hath laid on him the iniquity of us all</u>.

## John 10:17-18 (KJV)

[17] Therefore doth my Father love me, because <u>I lay down my life</u>, that I might take it again.

[18] No man taketh it from me, but <u>I lay it down of myself</u>. I have power to lay it down, and I have power to take it again. This commandment have I received of my Father.

## Hebrews 9:26 (KJV)

[26] For then must he often have suffered since the foundation of the world: but now once in the end of the world hath <u>he appeared to put away sin by the sacrifice of himself</u>.

## Matthew 26:28 (KJV)

[28] For <u>this is my blood of the new testament</u>, <u>which is shed for many for the remission of sins</u>.

## Hebrews 2:9 (KJV)

[9] But we see <u>Jesus</u>, who was made a little lower than the angels for the suffering of death, crowned with glory and honour; that he by the grace of God <u>should taste death for every man</u>.

## Romans 1:4 (KJV)

[4] And <u>declared *to be* the Son of God</u> with power, according to the spirit of holiness, <u>by the resurrection from the dead</u>:

## Romans 6:23 (KJV)

[23] For <u>the wages of sin *is* death</u>; but <u>the gift of God *is* eternal life through Jesus Christ our Lord</u>.

**Jesus had the supernatural power to put our sin natures, our satanic spiritual DNA lives, on the cross in Him, to crucify and to destroy those sin natures. The night before the day Jesus was crucified, and just before going to the garden of Gethsemane, Jesus spoke to God the Father.**

## John 17:1-2 (KJV)

[1] These words spake Jesus, and lifted up his eyes to heaven, and said, Father, the hour is come; glorify thy Son, that thy Son also may glorify thee:

[2] As thou hast given him power over all flesh, that he should give eternal life to as many as thou hast given him.

Receiving eternal life with God is only possible by being born again. God the Father had given Jesus the supernatural power over all peoples to destroy their satanic spiritual DNA lives, their sin natures, as the first step in them being born again. We can't have second, new spiritual DNA lives when our first satanic spiritual DNA lives still exist.

## Galatians 2:20 (KJV)

[20] I am crucified with Christ: nevertheless I live; yet not I, but Christ liveth in me: and the life which I now live in the flesh I live by the faith of the Son of God, who loved me, and gave himself for me.

Our crucifixion with Jesus did not destroy our physical lives ("nevertheless I live") but destroyed our satanic spiritual DNA lives, our sin natures.

## Romans 6:3 (KJV)

[3] Know ye not, that so many of us as were baptized into Jesus Christ were baptized into his death?

## Romans 6:6 (KJV)

[6] Knowing this, that our old man is crucified with *him*, that the body of sin might be destroyed, that henceforth we should not serve sin.

Our satanic spiritual DNA life, our "old man," our sin nature, had to die for us to be able to receive new spiritual DNA, from our new spiritual Father, God.

Our physical bodies are the instruments by which we perform physical activities. For example, we use our mouths and tongues to speak words. Our spiritual bodies, our sin natures, are the basis for us to sin. For example, having lying spirits, we choose, when tempted, to speak lies. Without our mouths and tongues, we would not speak. Without lying spirits, we would not speak lies.

In this way, we can understand how the scripture speaks of our old man as the body of sin which is destroyed by crucifixion. The penalty for sin is death (Romans 6:23). Our sin natures died in Jesus when He was crucified and no longer have the legal right to dominate us in the spiritual realm. Jesus' death paid the spiritual, legal penalties for all our sins, creating a spiritual, legal reality whereby we are released from the spiritual prison of our sin natures. Moreover, we can never be legally, spiritually tried again.

Ultimately, our new spiritual reality is that our sin natures are dead, which frees us from the law of sin and from being the servants of sin.

Scripture describes this as being similar to the death of a husband, representing our sin natures, which results in his widowed wife being freed from the marital law (the law of her husband) since she is no longer married to him. Similar to the widow, who is now legally free to remarry, when our sin natures are dead, we are free from the law of sin which allows for us to be legally married to another, Jesus Christ. The marriage to Jesus is a marriage covenant. The Christian Church is the Bride of Christ.

## Romans 7:1-4 (KJV)

¹ Know ye not, brethren, (for I speak to them that know the law,) how that the law hath dominion over a man as long as he liveth?
² For the woman which hath an husband is bound by the law to

*her* husband so long as he liveth; but <u>if the husband be dead, she is loosed from the law of *her* husband</u>.

³ So then if, while *her* husband liveth, she be married to another man, she shall be called an adulteress: but <u>if her husband be dead, she is free from that law</u>; so that she is no adulteress, though she be married to another man.

⁴ Wherefore, my brethren, ye also are become dead to the law by the body of Christ; that <u>ye should be married to another, *even* to him who is raised from the dead</u>, that <u>we should bring forth fruit unto God</u>.

## Romans 8:2 (KJV)

² For <u>the law of the Spirit of life in Christ Jesus hath made me free from the law of sin</u> and death.

## Matthew 22:2 (KJV)

² <u>The kingdom of heaven</u> is like unto <u>a certain king</u>, which <u>made a marriage for his son</u>,

## Revelation 19:7 (KJV)

⁷ Let us be glad and rejoice, and give honour to him: for <u>the marriage of the Lamb is come</u>, <u>and his wife hath made herself ready</u>.

## Revelation 19:9 (KJV)

⁹ And he saith unto me, Write, Blessed *are* they which are called unto <u>the marriage supper of the Lamb</u>. And he saith unto me, These are the true sayings of God.

**As sinners, we are married to our sin natures and the offspring or fruit of those unions are sins. Once born again, we are married to Jesus Christ and the offspring or fruit of those unions are acts of righteousness and holiness.**

## Romans 6:20-22 (KJV)

²⁰ For <u>when ye were the servants of sin</u>, ye were free from righteousness.

²¹ What <u>fruit</u> had ye then in those things whereof ye are now ashamed? for the end of those things *is* death.
²² But now <u>being made free from sin</u>, and become servants to God, <u>ye have your fruit unto holiness</u>, and the end everlasting life.

## Romans 6:17-18 (KJV)

¹⁷ But God be thanked, that <u>ye were the servants of sin</u>, but ye have obeyed from the heart that form of doctrine which was delivered you.
¹⁸ <u>Being then made free from sin,</u> <u>ye became the servants of righteousness</u>.

Jesus removed the legal right for Satan to have his spiritual DNA preeminent in us spiritually, which legally allowed God, the Father, to have His spiritual DNA preeminent in us spiritually. On the cross, Jesus shed His blood and offered up His body through death for us, and we, by faith, believe and receive the propitiation.

After our sin natures are dead, God the Father can give us new spiritual lives, new spiritual DNA. He can put within us His Holy Spirit, His spiritual DNA.

## Ezekiel 36:26-27 (KJV)

²⁶ A new heart also will I give you, and <u>a new spirit will I put within you</u>: and I will take away the stony heart out of your flesh, and I will give you an heart of flesh.
²⁷ And <u>I will put my spirit within you</u>, and cause you to walk in my statutes, and ye shall keep my judgments, and do *them*.

Ezekiel 36:27 states what is the promise of the Father, which Jesus tells us is the <u>baptism of the Holy Spirit</u>, the placing of His Spirit into us (rather than upon us) which results in our receiving the <u>new</u> spiritual DNA from our new spiritual Father, God. This is what Jesus was referring to when, in John 3:3 and John 3:5, He said that <u>we have to be</u>

**born again, that we have to be born of the Spirit**, to enter into His Kingdom.

## Luke 24:49 (KJV)
⁴⁹ And, behold, I send the <u>promise of my Father</u> upon you: but tarry ye in the city of Jerusalem, <u>until ye be endued with power from on high</u>.

## Acts 1:4-5 (KJV)
⁴ And, being assembled together with *them*, commanded them that they should not depart from Jerusalem, but wait for the <u>promise of the Father</u>, which, *saith he*, ye have heard of me.
⁵ For John truly baptized with water; but ye shall be <u>baptized with the Holy Ghost</u> not many days hence.

## Acts 2:33 (KJV)
³³ Therefore being by the right hand of God exalted, and <u>having received of the Father the promise of the Holy Ghost</u>, he hath shed forth this, which ye now see and hear.

## John 1:12-13 (KJV)
¹² But as many as received him, <u>to them gave he power to become the sons of God</u>, *even* <u>to them that believe</u> on his name:
¹³ <u>Which were born</u>, not of blood, nor of the will of the flesh, nor of the will of man, but <u>of God</u>.

God the Father told John the Baptist that Jesus was going to fulfill the promise of the Father, because He told him that Jesus was going to baptize with the Holy Spirit, thereby, giving the spiritual DNA of God, the Father, which was only made possible by the Son of God, Jesus, allowing Himself to be the sacrifice to atone for our sin.

## John 1:33-34 (KJV)
³³ And I knew him not: but <u>he that sent me to baptize with water</u>, the same said unto me, Upon whom thou shalt see the Spirit

descending, and remaining on him, the same <u>is he which baptizeth with the Holy Ghost</u>.

[34] And I saw, and bare record that this <u>is the Son of God</u>.

**All of the Old Covenant saints were never born again, because they never received the promise of the Father.**

## Hebrews 11:39-40 (KJV)

[39] And these all, having obtained a good report through faith, <u>received not the promise</u>:

[40] God having provided some better thing for us, that <u>they without us should not be made perfect</u>.

**All of the Old Covenant saints, by faith, had good reports, but none were a son or daughter of God with regard to spiritual DNA. All, having been born as sinners, were sons and daughters of Satan with regard to spiritual DNA. However, those with the spiritual DNA of Satan were either vessels of honor and mercy (children of the promise) or vessels of dishonor and wrath (children of the flesh).**

## Romans 9:21-23 (KJV)

[21] Hath not the potter power over the clay, of the same lump to make one <u>vessel unto honour</u>, and another unto <u>dishonour</u>?

[22] *What* if God, willing to shew *his* wrath, and to make his power known, endured with much longsuffering the <u>vessels of wrath</u> fitted to destruction:

[23] And that he might make known the riches of his glory on the <u>vessels of mercy</u>, which he had afore prepared unto glory,

**Only those who are the children of the <u>promise</u> are counted as children of God.**

## Romans 9:6-9 (KJV)

[6] Not as though the word of God hath taken none effect. For they *are* not all Israel, which are of Israel:

[7] Neither, because they are the seed of Abraham, *are they* all

children: but, In Isaac shall thy seed be called.

[8] That is, They which are the children of the flesh, these *are* not the children of God: but the children of the promise are counted for the seed.

[9] For this *is* the word of promise, At this time will I come, and Sara shall have a son.

Despite having the spiritual DNA of Satan, there were those who chose to believe in God, had faith, received the Word of the LORD, and did works that glorified Him. Thereby, they received good reports and, when given the choice, chose to trust in Jesus to be saved. These were vessels of honor and mercy. These were the Old Covenant saints, the children of the promise. The children of the promise ultimately received the spiritual DNA of God the Father, since the scripture calls them the children of God.

Having the spiritual DNA of Satan, there were those who chose not to believe in God, did not have faith, rejected the Word of the LORD, and did works that did not glorify Him. Thereby, they did not receive good reports and, when given the choice, chose not to trust in Jesus to be saved. These were vessels of dishonor and wrath. These were the children of the flesh.

None of the Old Covenant saints were made perfect. This is why the least in the Kingdom of God is greater than John the Baptist, the greatest Old Covenant prophet. It is because of the difference in the spiritual DNA.

## Luke 7:28 (KJV)

[28] For I say unto you, Among those that are born of women there is not a greater prophet than John the Baptist: but he that is least in the kingdom of God is greater than he.

[Note: In the New Testament, John the Baptist and his parents, Elizabeth and Zacharias, were all said to have been filled with the Holy Ghost (Luke 1:15, 41 & 67). This was not the same as having the baptism of the Holy Spirit in terms of the indwelling spiritual DNA of God the Father, since the Scriptures state that Jesus needed to be glorified (crucifixion, resurrection, and ascension to sit at the right hand of God, the Father) before the gift (Acts 2:38, 10:45) of the Holy Spirit could be given in that way.]

## John 7:39 (KJV)

[39] (But this spake he of the Spirit, which they that believe on him should receive: <u>for the Holy Ghost was not yet *given*; because that Jesus was not yet glorified</u>.)

The disciples James and John also manifested that they didn't know what manner of spirit they were, that they had the satanic spiritual DNA, not the indwelling Holy Spirit which came at Pentecost.

## Luke 9:51-56 (KJV)

[51] And it came to pass, when the time was come that he should be received up, he stedfastly set his face to go to Jerusalem,

[52] And sent messengers before his face: and they went, and entered into a village of the Samaritans, to make ready for him.

[53] And they did not receive him, because his face was as though he would go to Jerusalem.

[54] And <u>when his disciples James and John saw *this*, they said, Lord, wilt thou that we command fire to come down from heaven, and consume them, even as Elias did</u>?

[55] But <u>he turned, and rebuked them</u>, and said, <u>Ye know not what manner of spirit ye are of</u>.

[56] <u>For the Son of man is not come to destroy men's lives, but to save *them*</u>. And they went to another village.

When we have Satan's spiritual DNA, even knowing the law and the scriptures is not enough to be truly righteous and not enough to get us into Jesus' Kingdom.

## Matthew 5:20 (KJV)

[20] For I say unto you, That <u>except your righteousness shall exceed</u> <u>*the righteousness*</u> of the scribes and Pharisees, ye shall in no case enter into the kingdom of heaven.

Only Jesus' righteousness is true righteousness. We receive this when we are born again into His Kingdom.

Jesus accomplished the impossible in that He took us with the spiritual DNA of Satan and killed our satanic lives on the cross. He did that so that God the Father's spiritual DNA through the Holy Spirit <u>could be put into us</u> and transform us into God's children, the children of the promise. Thus, we are born again.

## 2 Peter 1:4 (KJV)

[4] Whereby are given unto us exceeding great and precious promises: that by these <u>ye might be partakers of the divine</u> <u>nature</u>, having escaped the corruption that is in the world through lust.

## Romans 8:14 (KJV)

[14] <u>For as many as are led by the Spirit of God, they are the sons</u> <u>of God</u>.

## Romans 8:16 (KJV)

[16] <u>The Spirit itself beareth witness with our spirit, that we are the</u> <u>children of God</u>:

## Galatians 3:26 (KJV)

[26] <u>For ye are all the children of God by faith in Christ Jesus</u>.

## 1 John 3:1 (KJV)

[1] Behold, <u>what manner of love the Father hath bestowed upon</u> <u>us, that we should be called the sons of God</u>: therefore the world knoweth us not, because it knew him not.

In the physical world, Adam is said to have come from God, meaning that he was the son of God.

## Luke 3:38 (KJV)
[38] Which was *the son* of Enos, which was *the son* of Seth, which was *the son* of <u>Adam, which was *the son* of God</u>.

However, Jesus was the first Son of God spiritually; He was the <u>firstborn</u> of many brethren. Jesus was born on the earth with the spiritual DNA of God, His Father - the Holy Spirit - in Him spiritually.

## Romans 8:29 (KJV)
[29] For whom he did foreknow, he also did predestinate *to be* conformed to the image of <u>his Son</u>, that <u>he might be the firstborn among many brethren</u>.

## Colossians 1:18 (KJV)
[18] And <u>he is</u> the head of the body, the church: who is the beginning, <u>the firstborn from the dead</u>; that in all *things* he might have the preeminence.

## Hebrews 12:23 (KJV)
[23] To the general assembly and <u>church of the firstborn</u>, which are written in heaven, and to God the Judge of all, and to the spirits of just men <u>made perfect</u>,

When we are born again, we follow after Jesus who was begotten (the first of many brethren) of the Father and who had the spiritual DNA of His Father. Jesus had a better name than the angels: Son of God, which He inherited.

## Hebrews 1:4-6 (KJV)
[4] Being made so much better than the angels, as <u>he hath by inheritance</u> obtained <u>a more excellent name than they</u>.
[5] For unto which of the angels said he at any time, <u>Thou art my Son, this day have I begotten thee</u>? And again, <u>I will be to him a</u>

Father, and he shall be to me a Son?

⁶ And again, when <u>he bringeth in the firstbegotten</u> into the world, he saith, And let all the angels of God worship him.

**We are <u>heirs</u> of salvation.**

## Hebrews 1:14 (KJV)

¹⁴ Are they not all ministering spirits, sent forth to minister for them who shall be <u>heirs of salvation</u>?

**When we are born again, having obtained the Holy Spirit, we become a son or daughter of God the Father. We should understand that in the spiritual realm, God the Father, our new Father, holds us in His loving arms and proclaims: "<u>Thou art my child</u>, <u>this day have I begotten thee</u>" and says, "<u>I will be to them a Father</u>, and <u>they shall be to me a son or daughter!</u>" God the Father says: "<u>This is my beloved child, in whom I am well pleased</u>." For we have been made perfect, when we have been born again by the baptism of the Holy Spirit, the fulfillment of God's promise, with God now in us spiritually. This is the <u>scriptural</u> definition of being perfect.**

## Hebrews 1:5 (KJV)

⁵ For unto which of the angels said he at any time, <u>Thou art my Son, this day have I begotten thee? And again, I will be to him a Father, and he shall be to me a Son?</u>

## Mark 1:11 (KJV)

¹¹ And there came a voice from heaven, *saying*, <u>Thou art my beloved Son, in whom I am well pleased</u>.

## Hebrews 11:39-40 (KJV)

³⁹ And these all, having obtained a good report through faith, <u>received not the promise</u>:

⁴⁰ God having provided some better thing for us, that they without us should not be <u>made perfect</u>.

## Matthew 5:48 (KJV)

[48] Be ye therefore <u>perfect</u>, even as your Father which is in heaven is <u>perfect</u>.

## Luke 6:40 (KJV)

[40] The disciple is not above his master: but <u>every one that is perfect shall be as his master</u>.

## Hebrews 10:14 (KJV)

[14] For by one offering <u>he hath perfected for ever them that are sanctified</u>.

This is our new spiritual identity, our identity in Christ Jesus. This is marvelous and cannot be over-emphasized. It is foundational. God is our Abba, our Dad (Mark 14:36; Rom. 8:15; Gal. 4:6).

Salvation, being born again, is not just about having all of our sins forgiven so as to be reconciled with God so that we do not receive the penalty for our sins. Jesus said we need to be born again and so be adopted (Romans 8:15) by God the Father, becoming His sons and daughters. We are not to live our Christian lives as sinners, struggling with habitual sinning and justifying it by thinking that Jesus' blood keeps covering our sins. We must not believe that our sinning is inevitable because, after all, we are sinners. We are to live resurrected lives as saints which manifest to the world that our spiritual DNA Father is God. When we are born again spiritually, we are changed from sinners to saints, from sinful to righteous in Christ. We receive Jesus and walk in Him.

## 2 Corinthians 5:21 (KJV)

[21] For he hath made him *to be* sin for us, who knew no sin; that <u>we might be made the righteousness of God in him</u>.

## Colossians 2:6 (KJV)

[6] As ye have therefore received Christ Jesus the Lord, *so* walk ye in him:

For in Jesus is the fullness of the Godhead, and we are complete in Him. Our sin natures are removed by the circumcision of Christ. We are buried by water immersion baptism and are risen alive unto God by faith with all of our sins forgiven.

## Colossians 2:9-13 (KJV)

[9] For in him dwelleth all the fulness of the Godhead bodily.

[10] And ye are complete in him, which is the head of all principality and power:

[11] In whom also ye are circumcised with the circumcision made without hands, in putting off the body of the sins of the flesh by the circumcision of Christ:

[12] Buried with him in baptism, wherein also ye are risen with *him* through the faith of the operation of God, who hath raised him from the dead.

[13] And you, being dead in your sins and the uncircumcision of your flesh, hath he quickened together with him, having forgiven you all trespasses;

Jesus had to fulfill His calling to be the sacrificial Lamb of God. He had to be crucified and resurrected and to ascend to the right hand of God the Father, or else the Promise of the Father, the Holy Spirit, the Comforter, could not be sent.

## John 16:7 (KJV)

[7] Nevertheless I tell you the truth; It is expedient for you that I go away: for if I go not away, the Comforter will not come unto you; but if I depart, I will send him unto you.

Jesus' time to be glorified finally arrived, and therefore, the Baptism of the Holy Spirit was soon to be possible. If we love our original, sin-filled lives, then we will eternally lose our lives and receive eternal death. If we hate our original, sin-filled lives, then we will repent of our sins, be born again, and receive eternal life. We are not called to hate and give up the gifts, talents, and desires with which God has gifted us. God made each of us unique and special. Each of us is designed and equipped to fulfill His various callings on our lives; these are our God-gifted destinies. However, like the corn of wheat, we need to have our sin-filled lives die, buried in water baptism, and then be resurrected into new spiritual lives in Christ with the Holy Spirit indwelling us and bringing forth much fruit which glorifies our new spiritual Father. We are to hate our original spiritual lives as sinners.

## John 12:23-25 (KJV)

[23] And Jesus answered them, saying, The hour is come, that <u>the Son of man should be glorified</u>.
[24] Verily, verily, I say unto you, <u>Except a corn of wheat fall into the ground and die</u>, it abideth alone: <u>but if it die</u>, <u>it bringeth forth much fruit</u>.
[25] <u>He that loveth his life shall lose it</u>; and <u>he that hateth his life in this world shall keep it unto life eternal</u>.

Let us now take a look at the complete birthing process of being born again.

# THE SPIRITUAL
# BIRTH CANAL

The Spiritual Birth Canal is a way of understanding the complete accomplishment of Jesus saving us and how we are fully born again to manifest that we are the children of God. The Spiritual Birth Canal consists of us having faith and believing in God, repenting of our sins, calling on Jesus to forgive us and be our Lord and Savior, having water immersion baptism, having Jesus baptize us with the Holy Spirit, and believing that spiritual power comes down from heaven on us from Jesus for us to live resurrected lives as children of God.

Having faith and believing in God means believing that we are sinners, that there will be a resurrection from the dead and an eternal judgment, and that God the Father sent Jesus to be our Savior. It means confessing that Jesus died on the cross for our sins, was buried, and was raised by God from the dead three days later and now sits alive at the right hand of God the Father.

Our salvation starts with believing in God, having faith, and receiving the Word of God, for we are saved through faith.

## Ephesians 2:8 (KJV)
[8] For by grace <u>are ye saved through faith</u>; and that not of yourselves: *it is* <u>the gift of God</u>:

## John 3:16 (KJV)

[16] For God so loved the world, that he gave his only begotten Son, that whosoever believeth in him should not perish, but have everlasting life.

## Romans 10:8-10 (KJV)

[8] But what saith it? The word is nigh thee, *even* in thy mouth, and in thy heart: that is, the word of faith, which we preach;
[9] That if thou shalt confess with thy mouth the Lord Jesus, and shalt believe in thine heart that God hath raised him from the dead, thou shalt be saved.
[10] For with the heart man believeth unto righteousness; and with the mouth confession is made unto salvation.

**Through the supernatural work of the Holy Spirit, we believe that we are sinners and need a savior whom the Holy Spirit reveals to be Jesus. We are convicted of our sinful nature and repent of our sins and call on Jesus, asking Him to forgive us and save us.**

## Romans 3:10 (KJV)

[10] As it is written, There is none righteous, no, not one:

## Romans 14:10-11 (KJV)

[10] But why dost thou judge thy brother? or why dost thou set at nought thy brother? for we shall all stand before the judgment seat of Christ.
[11] For it is written, *As* I live, saith the Lord, every knee shall bow to me, and every tongue shall confess to God.

## Mark 1:14-15 (KJV)

[14] Now after that John was put in prison, Jesus came into Galilee, preaching the gospel of the kingdom of God,
[15] And saying, The time is fulfilled, and the kingdom of God is at hand: repent ye, and believe the gospel.

## Romans 10:13 (KJV)

<sup>13</sup> For whosoever shall call upon the name of the Lord shall be saved.

## Acts 4:10-12 (KJV)

<sup>10</sup> Be it known unto you all, and to all the people of Israel, that by the name of Jesus Christ of Nazareth, whom ye crucified, whom God raised from the dead, *even* by him doth this man stand here before you whole.
<sup>11</sup> This is the stone which was set at nought of you builders, which is become the head of the corner.
<sup>12</sup> Neither is there salvation in any other: for there is none other name under heaven given among men, whereby we must be saved.

## Isaiah 43:11 (KJV)

<sup>11</sup> I, *even* I, *am* the LORD; and beside me *there is* no saviour.

## Isaiah 45:22-24 (KJV)

<sup>22</sup> Look unto me, and be ye saved, all the ends of the earth: for I *am* God, and *there is* none else.
<sup>23</sup> I have sworn by myself, the word is gone out of my mouth *in* righteousness, and shall not return, That unto me every knee shall bow, every tongue shall swear.
<sup>24</sup> Surely, shall *one* say, in the LORD have I righteousness and strength: *even* to him shall *men* come; and all that are incensed against him shall be ashamed.

## John 14:6 (KJV)

<sup>6</sup> Jesus saith unto him, I am the way, the truth, and the life: no man cometh unto the Father, but by me.

## Acts 2:36-39 (KJV)

<sup>36</sup> Therefore let all the house of Israel know assuredly, that God hath made that same Jesus, whom ye have crucified, both Lord and Christ.

³⁷ Now when they heard *this*, they were pricked in their heart, and said unto Peter and to the rest of the apostles, Men *and* brethren, what shall we do?

³⁸ Then Peter said unto them, <u>Repent, and be baptized every one of you in the name of Jesus Christ for the remission of sins, and ye shall receive the gift of the Holy Ghost</u>.

³⁹ For <u>the promise</u> is unto you, and to your children, and to all that are afar off, *even* as many as the Lord our God shall call.

**After we repent of our sins and call on Jesus to be our Lord and Savior, we have immersion water baptism, because our sin natures are dead and need to be buried with water baptism. Water baptism represents the acknowledgment that our old sin natures have been destroyed by Jesus on His cross. Water baptism acknowledges that dead things need to be buried and that all of our sins have been remitted, covered, and forgiven, by the shedding of the precious blood of Jesus Christ for us.**

## Romans 6:6 (KJV)

⁶ Knowing this, that <u>our old man is crucified with *him*</u>, that <u>the body of sin [spiritual DNA of Satan] might be destroyed</u>, that henceforth we should not serve sin.

## Hebrews 9:22 (KJV)

²² And almost <u>all things are by the law purged with blood</u>; and <u>without shedding of blood is no remission</u>.

## Hebrews 10:10-17 (KJV)

¹⁰ By the which will <u>we are sanctified through the offering of the body of Jesus Christ once *for all*</u>.

¹¹ And every priest standeth daily ministering and offering oftentimes the same sacrifices, which can never take away sins:

¹² But this man, <u>after he had offered one sacrifice for sins for ever</u>, sat down on the right hand of God;

¹³ From henceforth expecting till his enemies be made his footstool.

<sup>14</sup> For by one offering he hath perfected for ever them that are sanctified.

<sup>15</sup> *Whereof* the Holy Ghost also is a witness to us: for after that he had said before,

<sup>16</sup> This *is* the covenant that I will make with them after those days, saith the Lord, I will put my laws into their hearts, and in their minds will I write them;

<sup>17</sup> And their sins and iniquities will I remember no more.

In water immersion baptism, we are buried with Christ (under the water) and are risen with Christ (up out of the water) to represent our new spiritual life in Him. Jesus was physically crucified and buried. By faith, we believe that we were spiritually crucified with Him on the cross and, therefore, we bury ourselves by water immersion as a spiritual act. Jesus rose from the dead by the power of the Holy Spirit. By faith, we believe that our satanic spiritual DNA sin natures, wherein we were spiritually dead, have been destroyed on the cross and are buried in water baptism. In the waters of immersion baptism, our old sin-filled lives are done away with forever so that we, by the power of the Holy Spirit, can be resurrected from our spiritual deaths (coming up and out of our watery graves) and have new spiritual DNA lives (being born again in Jesus).

## Acts 22:16 (KJV)

<sup>16</sup> And now why tarriest thou? arise, and be baptized, and wash away thy sins, calling on the name of the Lord.

## Mark 16:16 (KJV)

<sup>16</sup> He that believeth and is baptized shall be saved; but he that believeth not shall be damned.

Water immersion baptism is the action that follows for those that believe. If we believe, knowing the scriptures, we get baptized through water immersion.

Once out of the water, we ask Jesus to <u>baptize us with the Holy Spirit</u> (the promise of God the Father) for <u>it is only Jesus who baptizes with the Holy Spirit</u>.

## John 1:29-34 (KJV)

[29] The next day John seeth Jesus coming unto him, and saith, <u>Behold the Lamb of God, which taketh away the sin of the world</u>.

[30] This is he of whom I said, After me cometh a man which is preferred before me: for he was before me.

[31] And I knew him not: but that he should be made manifest to Israel, therefore am I come baptizing with water.

[32] And John bare record, saying, I saw the Spirit descending from heaven like a dove, and it abode upon him.

[33] And I knew him not: but he that sent me to baptize with water, the same said unto me, <u>Upon whom thou shalt see the Spirit descending, and remaining on him, the same is he which baptizeth with the Holy Ghost</u>.

[34] And I saw, and bare record that <u>this is the Son of God</u>.

## Acts 1:5 (KJV)

[5] For John truly baptized with water; but <u>ye shall be baptized with the Holy Ghost</u> not many days hence.

After Jesus <u>baptizes us with the Holy Spirit</u>, <u>power comes down on us</u> to live our new, resurrected, spiritual lives.

## Acts 2:1, 4 (KJV)

[1] And when the day of Pentecost was fully come, they were all with one accord in one place.

[4] And <u>they were all filled with the Holy Ghost, and began to speak with other tongues</u>, as the Spirit gave them utterance.

## Acts 10:24 (KJV)

[24] And the morrow after they entered into Caesarea. And Cornelius waited for them, and had called together his kinsmen and near friends.

## Acts 10:44-47 (KJV)

<sup>44</sup> While Peter yet spake these words, the <u>Holy Ghost fell on all them</u> which heard the word.

<sup>45</sup> And they of the circumcision which believed were astonished, as many as came with Peter, because that <u>on the Gentiles also was poured out the gift of the Holy Ghost</u>.

<sup>46</sup> <u>For they heard them speak with tongues</u>, and magnify God. Then answered Peter,

<sup>47</sup> Can any man forbid water, that these should not be baptized, <u>which have received the Holy Ghost</u> as well as we?

## 1 Corinthians 4:20 (KJV)

<sup>20</sup> For <u>the kingdom of God *is*</u> not in word, but <u>in power</u>.

## Acts 1:8 (KJV)

<sup>8</sup> But <u>ye shall receive power</u>, <u>after that the Holy Ghost is come upon you</u>: and ye shall be witnesses unto me both in Jerusalem, and in all Judaea, and in Samaria, and unto the uttermost part of the earth.

The baptism of the Holy Spirit is essential for us to receive the spiritual power which we need to live the resurrected life. Having the Holy Spirit in some way is not enough; we need to receive the promise of the Father, the baptism of the Holy Spirit. It is recorded that, on the night Jesus first rose from the dead, He breathed on his disciples and said, "Receive ye the Holy Ghost." This was not the baptism of the Holy Spirit which occurred seven weeks later at Pentecost.

## John 20:19-22 (KJV)

<sup>19</sup> Then <u>the same day at evening</u>, being the first *day* of the week, when the doors were shut where <u>the disciples were assembled for fear of the Jews</u>, <u>came Jesus and stood in the midst</u>, and saith unto them, Peace *be* unto you.

[20] And when he had so said, he shewed unto them *his* hands and his side. Then were the disciples glad, when they saw the Lord.
[21] Then said Jesus to them again, Peace *be* unto you: as *my* Father hath sent me, even so send I you.
[22] And when he had said this, <u>he breathed on *them*, and saith unto them, Receive ye the Holy Ghost</u>:

The disciples' behavior after Jesus' resurrection and before Pentecost consisted of assembling to pray (Acts 1:13-14), worshipping Jesus (Matthew 28:17), traveling (Luke 24:13), and fishing (John 21:3). After having the baptism of the Holy Spirit at Pentecost, the disciples were preaching the Gospel in the public square, healing the sick, doing miracles, raising the dead, and casting out demons (Mark 16:20 & The Book of Acts).

To fully manifest the spiritual resurrection from the spiritual death on the cross, we need to have the power given to us from God which comes after the baptism of the Holy Spirit. This is similar to Jesus physically manifesting that He is the Son of God.

## Romans 1:3-4 (KJV)

[3] Concerning <u>his Son Jesus Christ our Lord</u>, which was made of the seed of David according to the flesh;
[4] And <u>declared *to be* the Son of God with power</u>, <u>according to the spirit of holiness</u>, <u>by the resurrection from the dead</u>:

As born-again believers in Jesus Christ, our new spiritual lives should reflect <u>the power</u> of the Holy Spirit manifested in our being made perfect: we have new spiritual natures. We have God's nature, which is full of holiness and righteousness. We <u>choose</u> to obey God rather than to choose to sin, and we have been resurrected from spiritual death. By this, we <u>declare</u> to the natural and supernatural worlds that we are the <u>sons and daughters of God</u>.

## Romans 8:11 (KJV)

[11] But if <u>the Spirit of him that raised up Jesus from the dead dwell in you</u>, he that raised up Christ from the dead shall also quicken your mortal bodies <u>by his Spirit that dwelleth in you</u>.

The Holy Spirit raised Jesus from His physical death. The Holy Spirit raises us from our spiritual deaths. Once born again, we are in Christ Jesus with the spiritual DNA of God, our Father, in us; we walk in the Spirit with a new spiritual life in Christ Jesus; and we come under a new law, which is <u>the law of the Spirit of life</u>.

## Romans 8:1-2 (KJV)

[1] *There is* therefore now no condemnation to them which are <u>in Christ Jesus, who walk not after the flesh, but after the Spirit.</u>
[2] For <u>the law of the Spirit of life in Christ Jesus hath made me free from the law of sin and death</u>.

The flesh represents the sin nature and signifies our condition before being born again. With the flesh, we serve the law of sin.

## Romans 7:23 (KJV)

[23] But I see another law in my members, warring against the law of my mind, and bringing me into captivity to <u>the law of sin</u> which is in my members.

## Romans 7:25 (KJV)

[25] I thank God through Jesus Christ our Lord. So then with the mind I myself serve the law of God; but <u>with the flesh the law of sin</u>.

It is imperative to understand that once we are born again, <u>we can still choose to sin</u>; we still have free will, but it is no longer in our spiritual DNA's nature to use our free will to sin. God specifically tells us not to choose to live the way we had prior to being born again. God instructs us to mortify the deeds of the body; to walk in the Spirit; not to walk in the flesh; to reckon ourselves dead to sinning; to put on the new man, which has the spiritual DNA of God; and to take off the old man, which has the spiritual DNA of Satan.

## Romans 8:13-14 (KJV)
[13] For if ye live after the flesh, ye shall die: but <u>if ye through the Spirit do mortify the deeds of the body, ye shall live</u>.
[14] <u>For as many as are led by the Spirit of God, they are the sons of God</u>.

## Romans 6:11 (KJV)
[11] Likewise <u>reckon ye also yourselves to be dead indeed unto sin</u>, but alive unto God through Jesus Christ our Lord.

## Romans 13:14 (KJV)
[14] But <u>put ye on the Lord Jesus Christ</u>, and make not provision for the flesh, to *fulfil* the lusts *thereof.*

## Galatians 3:27 (KJV)
[27] For as many of you <u>as have been baptized into Christ have put on Christ</u>.

## Ephesians 4:22 (KJV)
[22] That ye <u>put off </u>concerning the former conversation <u>the old man</u>, which is corrupt according to the deceitful lusts;

## Ephesians 4:24 (KJV)
[24] And that ye <u>put on the new man</u>, which after God is <u>created in righteousness and true holiness</u>.

## Colossians 3:9-10 (KJV)
[9] Lie not one to another, seeing that ye have <u>put off the old man</u> with his deeds;
[10] And have <u>put on the new *man*</u>, which is renewed in knowledge after the image of him that created him:

The following analogy is to help us understand the complete spiritual transformation which occurs when we are born again and are no longer sinners but are New Covenant saints whose spiritual new natures are to choose not to sin.

An American baseball player named, John, is under legal contract with a baseball team named the Hellcats. Every winter, John receives an email informing him when and where to appear for the new season's baseball spring training. However, at the end of last year's baseball season, his contract with the Hellcats expired, and the team's management did not renew John's baseball contract. Because of an error, the usual email informing John about spring training is sent to him. John goes to the spring training camp and enters the baseball players' locker room. There he finds his prior teammates who say to him, "John, what are you doing here? You don't have to be here and play baseball. You're a FREE AGENT!" John then realizes that he is no longer under contract and, therefore, no longer under the authority of the Hellcats' baseball organization. He recognizes that he does not have to play baseball for them. He says, "You're right!" and leaves the training camp.

Our previous sin habits may lead us to be tempted to sin, but being no longer servants of sin, we can choose not to sin. We no longer have a contract with Satan. Jesus legally frees us so that we are under contract with God and choose to obey His orders instead of our flesh. This contract is a covenant made in love.

## John 8:36 (KJV)
[36] If the Son therefore shall make you free, ye shall be free indeed.

## Galatians 5:1 (KJV)
[1] Stand fast therefore in the liberty wherewith Christ hath made us free, and be not entangled again with the yoke of bondage.

Once freed from our old sin natures and having new spiritual DNA natures, we can and should naturally <u>choose</u> to listen to <u>the Holy Spirit leading us</u> and to walk in Him. God tells us <u>not to let sin reign in us</u> which He would not do, if we were still servants of sin; for that would be as futile as telling a dog, whose nature is to bark, not to bark.

To further understand the tremendous significance of being born again in regard to sinning, we can use the analogy of dogs as unsaved sinners and cats as born again believers. We could say that the dog's natural behavior is to chase cars, but the cat's natural behavior is not to chase cars. When the dog is transformed into a cat, the new cat sees a car going down the street but no longer feels inclined to chase after it, because it is a new creature whose nature is not to chase cars. We could ask the cat, "Don't you want to chase the car?", and the cat (if it could talk) would say, "No – that hardly crossed my mind." A cat sees a car going by it but chooses not to chase it. Born-again believers can choose to sin, but doing so is no longer spiritually natural for them. Sinning is no longer a natural behavior. Born-again believers are new spiritual creatures.

## 2 Corinthians 5:17 (KJV)
[17] Therefore <u>if any man *be* in Christ</u>, *he is* <u>a new creature</u>: <u>old things are passed away</u>; behold, <u>all things are become new</u>.

## Romans 8:16 (KJV)
[16] The <u>Spirit itself beareth witness with our spirit, that we are the children of God</u>:

## Romans 6:3-7 (KJV)
[3] Know ye not, that so many of us as were <u>baptized into Jesus Christ were baptized into his death</u>?
[4] Therefore <u>we are buried with him by baptism into death</u>: that <u>like as Christ was raised up from the dead</u> by the glory of the Father, even so we also <u>should walk in newness of life</u>.

⁵ For <u>if we have been planted together in the likeness of his death,</u> <u>we shall be also</u> *in the likeness* of *his* <u>resurrection:</u>
⁶ Knowing this, that <u>our old man is crucified with</u> *him*, that <u>the</u> <u>body of sin might be destroyed,</u> that <u>henceforth we should not</u> <u>serve sin.</u>
⁷ For <u>he that is dead</u> is <u>freed from sin.</u>

## Romans 6:11-13 (KJV)

¹¹ Likewise <u>reckon ye also yourselves to be dead indeed unto sin,</u> <u>but alive unto God through Jesus Christ our Lord.</u>
¹² <u>Let not sin therefore reign in your mortal body,</u> that ye should obey it in the lusts thereof.
¹³ <u>Neither yield ye your members</u> *as* <u>instruments of</u> <u>unrighteousness unto sin:</u> <u>but yield yourselves unto God, as those</u> <u>that are alive from the dead,</u> and your members *as* instruments of righteousness unto God.

## Romans 6:18-22 (KJV)

¹⁸ <u>Being then made free from sin, ye became the servants of</u> <u>righteousness.</u>
¹⁹ I speak after the manner of men because of the infirmity of your flesh: for as ye have yielded your members servants to uncleanness and to iniquity unto iniquity; even so now <u>yield your</u> <u>members servants to righteousness unto holiness.</u>
²⁰ For when ye were the servants of sin, ye were free from righteousness.
²¹ What fruit had ye then in those things whereof ye are now ashamed? for the end of those things *is* death.
²² But now <u>being made free from sin,</u> and <u>become servants to</u> <u>God,</u> ye have your fruit unto holiness, and <u>the end everlasting</u> <u>life.</u>

## 1 John 3:5-10 (KJV)

⁵ And ye know that <u>he was manifested to take away our sins;</u> and <u>in him is no sin.</u>

⁶ <u>Whosoever abideth in him sinneth not</u>: whosoever sinneth hath not seen him, neither known him.

⁷ <u>Little children, let no man deceive you</u>: he that doeth righteousness is righteous, even as he is righteous.

⁸ <u>He that committeth sin is of the devil</u>; for the devil sinneth from the beginning. <u>For this purpose the Son of God was manifested, that he might destroy the works of the devil</u>.

⁹ <u>Whosoever is born of God doth not commit sin</u>; for his seed remaineth in him: and <u>he cannot sin, because he is born of God</u>.

¹⁰ <u>In this the children of God are manifest, and the children of the devil</u>: whosoever doeth not righteousness is not of God, neither he that loveth not his brother.

We need to be fully born again and not get stuck, as it were, in the Spiritual Birth Canal of salvation. There are some Christians who have believed in God, repented of their sins, and received the Holy Spirit in some way, similar to the disciples the first evening after Jesus' resurrection, but they appear to live their Christian lives like Old Covenant saints. They have a "heart after God's own heart," but, like King David who committed adultery and killed a woman's husband, they continue to struggle with besetting sins. Their <u>identities</u> as Christians are still those of sinners, but of sinners saved by grace. They manifest no resurrection power. Being born again includes not only believing in God and repenting of our sins but also having water immersion baptism and being baptized with the Holy Spirit with the power coming down afterward. We should not get stuck in the born-again Spiritual Birth Canal. We should also understand the salvation package in order to preach the Gospel so that others will be fully born again and not be frustrated by being stuck in the Spiritual Birth Canal.

We are spiritually fully born again by entering and fully exiting the Spiritual Birth Canal of Jesus' new birth which enables us to know who we are in Christ and to spiritually walk in that new and true identity. We must have faith and believe in God; repent of our sins; call on Jesus to forgive us; have water immersion baptism; have Jesus baptize us with the Holy Spirit; and believe that spiritual power comes down from Heaven on us from Jesus who is sitting at the right hand of God the Father with the power given to us for us to live resurrected lives as children of God.

Salvation is part of the foundational principles of the Doctrine of Christ (Hebrews 6:1-2; 2 John 1:9) which are 1) repentance from dead works (sins), 2) having faith toward God, 3) the doctrine of baptism (water immersion and of the Holy Spirit; John 3:5), 4) the laying on of hands (healing the sick: Mark 16:18; receiving the baptism of the Holy Spirit: Acts 19:6), 5) resurrection of the dead (Revelation 20:12-13) and 6) eternal judgment (2 Corinthians 5:10, Romans 14:10).

Here is an example of "How to" steps to receiving salvation:

Repent of Sins: "Lord, I am a sinner. Please forgive me of my sins (demonstrates repentance from dead works) and save me from the wrath to come (acknowledges resurrection and eternal judgment). Come into my heart. I call on you, Jesus, and make you my Lord and my Savior. I believe (shows faith towards God) that you died on the cross for my sins, were buried, and were raised from the dead by God three days later and now sit alive at the right hand of God, the Father."

Water Immersion Baptism:

Under the water – think, "I am buried with Christ!"

Up out of the water – think, "I am risen with Christ!"

Baptism of the Holy Spirit:

Say out loud, "Jesus, please Baptize me with the Holy Spirit with the evidence of speaking in tongues."

Speak as the Holy Spirit gives you utterance. The Holy Spirit will not override your will and force you to speak, so you must choose to speak.

Power from Jesus:

After the Baptism of the Holy Spirit, believe and know that Power has come down on you from Jesus to live the resurrected life in Christ.

When we choose not to get baptized with water immersion or choose not to be baptized by Jesus with the Holy Spirit, we choose to have a life that misses major foundational aspects of the Doctrine of Christ.

# OLD VERSUS NEW COVENANT SAINTS

The difference between Old and New Covenant saints is as distinct as night and day, as death and life. What Jesus accomplished on earth with His obedient life, death on the cross, resurrection from the dead, and ascension into heaven can't be overstated. He did what allows for all to be born again.

Before comparing Old versus New Covenant saints, let us first briefly look at the Old and New Covenants. The Old Covenant was made with the Jewish people starting with Abraham [Genesis 17:1-7], the father of Isaac, who was the father of Jacob who was called Israel. The New Covenant was also made with the Jewish people (Hebrews 8:6-13, Romans 9:4) and was a completion of the Old Covenant. The non-Jewish peoples, the Gentiles (Ephesians 2:11-19) became part of the New Covenant by being metaphorically "grafted into the olive tree" of the Jewish Covenant (Romans 11:17, 24).

Jesus' appearance on earth as the Godman was the beginning of the fulfillment of God's promise to the Jewish people that He was going to give them a New Covenant (Ezekiel 37: 26-27) in exchange for the Old Covenant. It may be that God communicated to the Jewish people the transition from Old to New Covenant when Jesus was transfigured on a high mountain:

## Mark 9:2-7 (KJV)

² And after six days <u>Jesus</u> taketh *with him* <u>Peter, and James, and John</u>, and leadeth them up into an high mountain apart by

themselves: and he was <u>transfigured before them</u>.

³ And his raiment became shining, exceeding white as snow; so as no fuller on earth can white them.

⁴ And there appeared unto them <u>Elias with Moses</u>: and they were talking with Jesus.

⁵ And <u>Peter</u> answered and <u>said to Jesus</u>, Master, it is good for us to be here: and <u>let us make three tabernacles; one for thee, and one for Moses, and one for Elias</u>.

⁶ For he wist not what to say; for they were sore afraid.

⁷ And <u>there was a cloud that overshadowed them: and a voice came out of the cloud, saying, This is my beloved Son: hear him</u>.

## Hebrews 1:1-2 (KJV)

¹ <u>God</u>, who at sundry times and in divers manners <u>spake in time past unto the fathers by the prophets</u>,

² Hath <u>in these last days spoken unto us by *his* Son</u>, whom he hath appointed heir of all things, by whom also he made the worlds;

Moses represents the Law of the Old Covenant, and Elijah represents all the prophets of the Old Covenant. Jesus represents the New Covenant. Peter, James, and John represent the Jewish people, with two or more witnesses being needed to establish a matter as true. Peter equates Jesus, Moses, and Elijah as <u>equal authorities</u> by asking Jesus to let them make three tabernacles, one for each person. However, God the Father says, "This is my beloved Son: hear him." This event appears to be a transition point; God has sent the Messiah, His Son, as promised, and is in the process of fulfilling His promise of a New Covenant when His Spirit would be placed in them.

Now let us compare Old versus New Covenant saints. The Old Covenant saints were those who by faith believed God, did works which glorified Him and thereby got good reports. However, they all were waiting for the promise of the Father to occur and were spiritually in Satan's kingdom.

## Hebrews 11:39-40 (KJV)

<sup>39</sup> And these all, <u>having obtained a good report through faith,</u> <u>received not the promise:</u>

<sup>40</sup> God having provided some better thing for us, <u>that they</u> without us <u>should not be made perfect.</u>

New Covenant saints receive the promise of the Father by faith, are born again, and spiritually enter into God's Kingdom. By implication (Hebrews 11:40), compared to Old Covenant saints, New Covenant saints are made perfect - meaning that they have received the Baptism of the Holy Spirit and have new spiritual DNA from their new Father.

## Galatians 3:14 (KJV)

<sup>14</sup> That the blessing of Abraham might come on the Gentiles through Jesus Christ; that we might receive <u>the promise of the</u> <u>Spirit through faith</u>.

## Hebrews 10:14 (KJV)

<sup>14</sup> For by one offering he hath <u>perfected</u> for ever them that are sanctified.

## Colossians 1:13 (KJV)

<sup>13</sup> Who hath delivered us from the power of darkness, and <u>hath</u> <u>translated *us* into the kingdom of his dear Son</u>:

The Old Covenant saints' thoughts and ways were not God's thoughts and ways.

## Hebrews 3:9-10 (KJV)

<sup>9</sup> When <u>your fathers</u> tempted me, proved me, and saw my works forty years.

<sup>10</sup> Wherefore I was grieved with that generation, and said, They do alway err in *their* heart; and <u>they have not known my ways</u>.

## John 8:23 (KJV)

23 And he said unto them, Ye are from beneath; I am from above: ye are of this world; I am not of this world.

## Isaiah 55:6-9 (KJV)

6 Seek ye the LORD while he may be found, call ye upon him while he is near:
7 Let the wicked forsake his way, and the unrighteous man his thoughts: and let him return unto the LORD, and he will have mercy upon him; and to our God, for he will abundantly pardon.
8 For my thoughts *are* not your thoughts, neither *are* your ways my ways, saith the LORD.
9 For *as* the heavens are higher than the earth, so are my ways higher than your ways, and my thoughts than your thoughts.

Christians who refer to the Old Covenant scriptures of Isaiah 55:8-9 to define their current New Covenant relationship with God should consider the preceding verses of Isaiah 55:6-7. These verses speak to the wicked and speak that they should repent of their thoughts and ways and seek the Lord for salvation while He is near. Chapter 55 of Isaiah is a salvation chapter: "Incline your ear unto me: hear, and your soul shall live; and I will make an everlasting covenant with you, ..." (verse 3); "Seek ye the LORD while he may be found, call ye upon him while he is near:" (verse 6); "...let him [the wicked] return unto the LORD, and he will have mercy upon him; and to our God, for he will abundantly pardon" (verse 7).

But New Covenant saints have the mind of Christ and the laws of God written on their minds and hearts. New Covenant saints think and behave like their Father, who works in them to desire His will and enables them to do it (Phil. 2:13). New Covenant saints had sin natures before being born again but have righteous natures after salvation. It is natural for them to do righteousness and not natural for them to sin. After being born again and becoming a child of

God, His thoughts and ways <u>are</u> their thoughts and ways. New Covenant saints walk in the <u>Holy</u> Spirit and discard any thoughts they discern as of their flesh or from evil spirits.

When born-again believers walk in the flesh and do not walk by faith in the Holy Spirit, then their thoughts are not God's thoughts and their ways are not God's ways. During that time, God may tell them that their thoughts and ways are not His so that they will turn from sin, mortify the flesh, put off the old man, put on the new man, and walk in the Holy Spirit.

## 1 Corinthians 2:16 (KJV)
[16] For who hath known the mind of the Lord, that he may instruct him? But <u>we have the mind of Christ</u>.

## Philippians 2:5 (KJV)
[5] <u>Let this mind be in you, which was also in Christ Jesus</u>:

## 2 Timothy 1:7 (KJV)
[7] For <u>God hath</u> not <u>given us</u> the spirit of fear; but of power, and of love, and of <u>a sound mind</u>.

## Hebrews 8:10 (KJV)
[10] For <u>this *is* the covenant</u> that I will make with the house of Israel after those days, saith the Lord; <u>I will put my laws into their mind, and write them in their hearts</u>: and I will be to them a God, and they shall be to me a people:

## Hebrews 10:16 (KJV)
[16] <u>This *is* the covenant</u> that I will make with them after those days, saith the Lord, <u>I will put my laws into their hearts, and in their minds will I write them</u>;

## Philippians 2:13 (KJV)
[13] For <u>it is God which worketh in you both to will and to do of *his* good pleasure</u>.

Old Covenant saints were given the law. They tried to follow the law and worked at being righteous. They trained themselves to be kind, generous, and good overall. One of the most self-righteous Old Covenant saints was Job who because of all of his good works was righteous in his own eyes (Job 32:1).

Job had known God as the LORD (Yahweh [Hebrew]/ Jehovah [English]) because Job "feared God" (Job 1:1 & Job 2:3) which was good (Proverbs 1:7; Luke 12:5). For example, Job knew the governmental aspect of the LORD (the spiritual law of seed, plant, and harvest [Genesis 8:22, Deuteronomy 28; Galatians 6:7; Matthew 9:38]) and that if his children sowed cursing God, that they would reap a bad harvest. So Job offered burnt offerings for them in case they did curse God so as to block the potential bad harvest (Job 1:5). Job knew God as LORD, but it appears he did not know Him as SAVIOR (Yah-Shua; translated literally, "Yahweh Saves"). Job trusted in his own righteousness to save himself but needed to trust Jesus to be saved, for there is no other name under heaven given among men whereby we must be saved (Acts 4:10-12). God tells Job that Job cannot save himself.

## Job 40:9 (KJV)
⁹ Hast thou an arm like God? or canst thou thunder with a voice like him?

## Job 40:14 (KJV)
¹⁴ Then will I also confess unto thee that thine own right hand can save thee.

Job wanted the LORD to answer him with regards to his own innocence (Job 31:6, 35). The LORD did show up (Job 38:1) and asked him where Job was when He, Jesus, laid the foundation of the earth (Job 38:4; Hebrews 1:10). Job was trusting in his own righteousness, but then he saw Jesus (Job

42:5 "I have heard of thee by the hearing of the ear: but now mine eye seeth thee"), the Son of God, having God the Father's spiritual DNA, the Holy Spirit. Then did Job realize that he, born a sinner, having satanic spiritual DNA, was therefore actually free from righteousness (Romans 6:20)? Seeing Jesus, Job saw salvation and eternal life (1 John 1:1-2). He thought of himself and repented (Job 42:6 "Wherefore I abhor myself, and repent in dust and ashes"). He must have then put his trust for his righteousness in Jesus and not in himself.

The best spiritual seed we can sow for our spiritual futures is to receive the Holy Spirit, the seed of the Father (1 John 3:9), to believe in God and be saved by Jesus. Then our spiritual eternal life is with God. If we don't sow that seed, the spiritual seeds that we sow for our spiritual futures are our sins, and our harvest is the just, wrath of God with eternal death in the lake of fire.

New Covenant saints are righteous and follow Jesus, led by the Holy Spirit, and are under the law of the Spirit of Life. New Covenant saints have God's laws put into their hearts and written in their minds. And, as they walk in the Spirit, they naturally fulfill the law's righteousness. New Covenant saints serve in newness of spirit and not in the oldness of the letter of the law. They have ceased working to be righteous but instead rest in Christ Jesus.

## John 1:17 (KJV)
[17] For the law was given by Moses, *but* grace and truth came by Jesus Christ.

## Romans 7:6 (KJV)
[6] But now we are delivered from the law, that being dead wherein we were held; that we should serve in newness of spirit, and not in the oldness of the letter.

## Romans 8:1-4 (KJV)

¹ *There is* therefore now no condemnation to them which are in Christ Jesus, who walk not after the flesh, but after the Spirit.

² For <u>the law of the Spirit of life in Christ Jesus hath made me free from the law of sin and death</u>.

³ For what the law could not do, in that it was weak through the flesh, God sending his own Son in the likeness of sinful flesh, and for sin, condemned sin in the flesh:

⁴ That <u>the righteousness of the law might be fulfilled in us</u>, <u>who walk</u> not after the flesh, but <u>after the Spirit</u>.

## Hebrews 10:16 (KJV)

¹⁶ This *is* the covenant that I will make with them after those days, saith the Lord, <u>I will put my laws into their hearts, and in their minds will I write them</u>;

## Romans 8:14 (KJV)

¹⁴ For <u>as many as are led by the Spirit of God, they are the sons of God</u>.

## Hebrews 4:6-10 (KJV)

⁶ Seeing therefore it remaineth that some must enter therein, and they to whom it was first preached <u>entered not in because of unbelief</u>:

⁷ Again, he limiteth a certain day, saying in David, To day, after so long a time; as it is said, To day if ye will hear his voice, harden not your hearts.

⁸ For if Jesus had given them rest, then would he not afterward have spoken of another day.

⁹ There remaineth therefore <u>a rest</u> to the people of God.

¹⁰ <u>For he that is entered into his rest</u>, <u>he also hath ceased from his own works</u>, as God *did* from his.

**Old Covenant saints had hard, stony hearts, but New Covenant saints have soft, fleshy hearts. New Covenant saints are not under the law, because Jesus fulfilled the law and**

blotted out the handwriting of ordinances that was against them and nailed it to His cross. The law is good and is for the lawless (1 Timothy 1:8-9); it is for those who have Satan's spiritual DNA, those with hard hearts.

## Ezekiel 11:19 (KJV)

[19] And I will give them one heart, and I will put a new spirit within you; and <u>I will take the stony heart</u> out of their flesh, <u>and will give them an heart of flesh</u>:

## Mark 10:2-5 (KJV)

[2] And the Pharisees came to him, and asked him, Is it lawful for a man to put away *his* wife? <u>tempting him</u>.
[3] And he answered and said unto them, <u>What did Moses command you</u>?
[4] And they said, Moses suffered to write a bill of divorcement, and to put *her* away.
[5] And Jesus answered and said unto them, <u>For the hardness of your heart</u> he wrote you this precept.

## Romans 6:14 (KJV)

[14] For sin shall not have dominion over you: <u>for ye are not under the law</u>, <u>but under grace</u>.

## Colossians 2:14 (KJV)

[14] <u>Blotting out the handwriting of ordinances that was against us</u>, which was contrary to us, <u>and took it out of the way</u>, <u>nailing it to his cross</u>;

Old Covenant saints were taught by Moses, prophets, kings, Pharisees and scribes.

New Covenant saints are taught by God the Father, Jesus, and the Holy Spirit.

## Hebrews 1:1-2 (KJV)

[1] God, who at sundry times and in divers manners <u>spake in time past unto the fathers by the prophets</u>,

[2] Hath <u>in these last days spoken unto us by *his* Son</u>, whom he hath appointed heir of all things, by whom also he made the worlds;

## Matthew 5:20 (KJV)

[20] For I say unto you, That <u>except your righteousness shall exceed *the righteousness* of the scribes and Pharisees</u>, ye shall in no case enter into the kingdom of heaven.

### Jeremiah 31:34 (KJV)

[34] And they shall teach no more every man his neighbour, and every man his brother, saying, Know the LORD: for <u>they shall all know me, from the least of them unto the greatest of them</u>, saith the LORD: for I will forgive their iniquity, and I will remember their sin no more.

## Hebrews 8:11-12 (KJV)

[11] And they shall not teach every man his neighbour, and every man his brother, saying, Know the Lord: <u>for all shall know me, from the least to the greatest</u>.

[12] For I will be merciful to their unrighteousness, and their sins and their iniquities will I remember no more.

## John 6:45 (KJV)

[45] It is written in the prophets, And <u>they shall be all taught of God</u>. Every man therefore that hath heard, and hath learned of the Father, cometh unto me.

## John 16:13 (KJV)

[13] Howbeit when he, <u>the Spirit of truth, is come, he will guide you into all truth</u>: for he shall not speak of himself; but whatsoever he shall hear, *that* shall he speak: and he will shew you things to come.

## 1 John 2:27 (KJV)

²⁷ But <u>the anointing [the Holy Spirit] which ye have received of him abideth in you, and ye need not that any man teach you: but as the same anointing teacheth you of all things</u>, and is truth, and is no lie, and even as it hath taught you, ye shall abide in him.

Old Covenant saints related to God with a separation between them and Him as represented by the veil separating them from the Ark of the Covenant in the most holy place in the tabernacle/temple.

New Covenant saints have a direct relationship with God, through the veil, and relate to Him as Abba Father because God has placed in their hearts the Spirit of His Son, Jesus.

## Exodus 26:33 (KJV)

³³ And <u>thou shalt hang up the vail</u> under the taches, that thou mayest bring in thither <u>within the vail the ark of the testimony: and the vail shall divide unto you between the holy *place* and the most holy</u>.

## Mark 15:38 (KJV)

³⁸ And <u>the veil of the temple was rent in twain from the top to the bottom</u>.

## Hebrews 10:19-20 (KJV)

¹⁹ <u>Having</u> therefore, brethren, <u>boldness to enter into the holiest by the blood of Jesus,</u>
²⁰ By a new and living way, which he hath consecrated for us, <u>through the veil</u>, that is to say, his flesh;

## Galatians 4:6 (KJV)

⁶ And <u>because ye are sons</u>, <u>God hath sent forth the Spirit of his Son into your hearts</u>, <u>crying</u>, <u>Abba</u>, <u>Father</u>.

Old Covenant saints wanted their enemies to be killed, sent quickly to hell, without mercy. They did not want their enemies' iniquity to be covered nor their sins blotted out.

## Psalm 54:5 (KJV)

[5] He shall reward evil unto mine enemies: <u>cut them off</u> in thy truth.

## Psalm 55:15 (KJV)

[15] <u>Let death seize upon them</u>, *and* <u>let them go down quick into hell</u>: for wickedness *is* in their dwellings, *and* among them.

## Psalm 59:1-5 (KJV)

[1] Deliver me from <u>mine enemies</u>, O my God: defend me from them that rise up against me.

[2] Deliver me from the workers of iniquity, and save me from bloody men.

[3] For, lo, they lie in wait for my soul: the mighty are gathered against me; not *for* my transgression, nor *for* my sin, O LORD.

[4] They run and prepare themselves without *my* fault: awake to help me, and behold.

[5] Thou therefore, O LORD God of hosts, the God of Israel, awake to visit all the heathen: <u>be not merciful to any wicked transgressors</u>. Selah.

## Nehemiah 4:4-5 (KJV)

[4] Hear, O our God; for we are despised: and turn their reproach upon their own head, and <u>give them for a prey in the land of captivity</u>:

[5] And <u>cover not their iniquity</u>, and <u>let not their sin be blotted out</u> from before thee: for they have provoked *thee* to anger before the builders.

New Covenant saints are to love their enemies, do good to them, be kind to them, be merciful to them, bless them, and pray for them. New Covenant saints are to be peacemakers.

## Luke 6:27 (KJV)

[27] But I say unto you which hear, <u>Love your enemies</u>, <u>do good to them</u> which hate you,

## Luke 6:35-36 (KJV)

[35] But <u>love ye your enemies, and do good</u>, and lend, hoping for nothing again; and your reward shall be great, and ye shall be the children of the Highest: for he is kind unto the unthankful and *to* the evil.
[36] <u>Be ye therefore merciful</u>, as your Father also is merciful.

## Matthew 5:44 (KJV)

[44] But I say unto you, <u>Love your enemies</u>, <u>bless them</u> that curse you, <u>do good to them</u> that hate you, and <u>pray for them</u> which despitefully use you, and persecute you;

## Matthew 5:9 (KJV)

[9] Blessed *are* the <u>peacemakers</u>: <u>for they shall be called the children of God</u>.

**For the Old Covenant saints, God was the LORD God, and they were the servants of the LORD. That was their spiritual <u>identity</u>. When the Old Covenant saints served the LORD God, that was their <u>behavior</u>.**

## Isaiah 41:8 (KJV)

[8] But thou, <u>Israel, *art* my servant, Jacob</u> whom I have chosen, the seed of Abraham my friend.

## Joshua 1:1 (KJV)

[1] Now after the death of <u>Moses the servant of the LORD</u> it came to pass, that the LORD spake unto Joshua the son of Nun, Moses' minister, saying,

## 2 Samuel 7:5 (KJV)

[5] Go and tell <u>my servant David</u>, Thus saith the LORD, Shalt thou build me an house for me to dwell in?

## 1 Kings 3:5-9 (KJV)

[5] In Gibeon <u>the LORD appeared to Solomon in a dream by night</u>: and God said, Ask what I shall give thee.

[6] And Solomon said, Thou hast shewed unto <u>thy servant David</u> my father great mercy, according as he walked before thee in truth, and in righteousness, and in uprightness of heart with thee; and thou hast kept for him this great kindness, that thou hast given him a son to sit on his throne, as *it is* this day.

[7] And now, O LORD my God, thou hast made <u>thy servant</u> king instead of David my father: and I *am but* a little child: I know not *how* to go out or come in.

[8] And <u>thy servant</u> *is* in the midst of thy people which thou hast chosen, a great people, that cannot be numbered nor counted for multitude.

[9] Give therefore <u>thy servant</u> an understanding heart to judge thy people, that I may discern between good and bad: for who is able to judge this thy so great a people?

**For New Covenant saints, God is our Father, (Matthew 6:9, Ephesians 1:3). We are His sons and daughters in whom He is well pleased, and we are part of God's family. This is our new spiritual <u>identity</u>. When New Covenant saints serve God, that is their <u>behavior</u>.**

## Galatians 4:4-7 (KJV)

[4] But when the fulness of the time was come, God sent forth his Son, made of a woman, made under the law,

[5] <u>To redeem them that were under the law</u>, that we might <u>receive the adoption of sons</u>.

[6] And because <u>ye are sons</u>, God hath sent forth the Spirit of his Son into your hearts, crying, Abba, Father.

[7] Wherefore <u>thou art no more a servant, but a son</u>; and if a son, then an heir of God through Christ.

**New Covenant saints are sons and daughters who serve God as a son or daughter would serve their father. Their**

relationship to God the Father is as family and not as household servants. The New Covenant scriptures repeatedly declare to the natural and supernatural realms that New Covenant saints are the sons and daughters of the Most High God, that they are part of His family, and that the Spirit of His Son has been sent by God into their hearts so that they can and do call Him Abba Father. For New Covenant saints, the Old Covenant "Our God" becomes "Our Father."

## John 20:17 (KJV)

<sup>17</sup> Jesus saith unto her, Touch me not; for I am not yet ascended to my Father: but <u>go to my brethren</u>, and say unto them, <u>I ascend unto my Father, and your Father</u>; and *to* my God, and your God.

## Matthew 6:9 (KJV)

<sup>9</sup> After this manner therefore <u>pray ye</u>: <u>Our Father which art in heaven</u>, Hallowed be thy name.

## Matthew 23:9 (KJV)

<sup>9</sup> And <u>call no *man* your father upon the earth: for one is your Father, which is in heaven</u>.

## 1 Corinthians 1:3 (KJV)

<sup>3</sup> Grace *be* unto you, and peace, from <u>God our Father</u>, and *from* the Lord Jesus Christ.

Each part of the Body of Christ, the Church, should be able to say, "If you have seen me, then you have seen the Father," because Jesus spiritually lives in New Covenant saints.

## John 14:9 (KJV)

<sup>9</sup> <u>Jesus saith</u> unto him, Have I been so long time with you, and yet hast thou not known me, Philip? <u>he that hath seen me hath seen the Father</u>; and how sayest thou *then*, Shew us the Father?

## Galatians 2:20 (KJV)

²⁰ I am crucified with Christ: nevertheless I live; yet not I, but <u>Christ liveth in me</u>: and the life which I now live in the flesh I live by the faith of the Son of God, who loved me, and gave himself for me.

Jesus said, "I am the Resurrection," and He lives in us. (Jesus never said, I am the crucifixion.) New Covenant saints should manifest that <u>they are the Resurrection</u> because the children of God are the children of the resurrection. God uses New Covenant saints to raise sinners from spiritual death into spiritual life through salvation in Jesus Christ, thus manifesting resurrection power. Jesus is the Resurrection, and that is why resurrection is such an integral part of salvation, confessing that God raised Jesus from the dead.

## John 11:25 (KJV)

²⁵ Jesus said unto her, <u>I am the resurrection</u>, and the life: he that believeth in me, though he were dead, yet shall he live:

## Philippians 3:10 (KJV)

¹⁰ That <u>I may know him, and the power of his resurrection</u>, and the fellowship of his sufferings, being made conformable unto his death;

## Luke 20:36 (KJV)

³⁶ Neither can they die any more: for they are equal unto the angels; and are <u>the children of God</u>, <u>being the children of the resurrection</u>.

## Romans 10:9 (KJV)

⁹ That if thou shalt <u>confess with thy mouth</u> the Lord Jesus, and shalt believe in thine heart that <u>God hath raised him from the dead, thou shalt be saved</u>.

New Covenant saints have a new spiritual birthright. They are born free when they are born again. The spiritual position of New Covenant saints is that they are heirs of God through Christ Jesus and are seated in Christ who sits on the seat of power to the right of God the Father. They walk in the Spirit, manifesting who their spiritual DNA Father is, even as Jesus walked on earth, doing the works His Father gave Him and saying the Words His Father spoke to and through Him. Jesus always manifested His identity as God's Son. New Covenant saints can respond to God the Father's Word in such a way that they appear by their behavior to be His slaves. But New Covenant saints choose not to use the language of slavery because slavery is associated with sin and darkness, and God is sinless and is light and in Him is no darkness. Slavery is one of the most unrighteous atrocities one man can inflict on another.

Jesus never said that He was God's slave.

New Covenant saints are to believe in God and no longer identify as sinners or slaves, but as children of God.

As born-again sons and daughters of God, New Covenant saints should study the Old Testament and the New Testament as the Holy Spirit leads them and should know them exceedingly well. However, viewing Old Covenant saints as the primary teachers of how New Covenant saints are to walk in the Spirit is suboptimal, since Old Covenant saints all had the spiritual DNA of Satan. None had been born again because Jesus had not yet been glorified. When New Covenant saints use the spiritual self-identity lens that they are sinners, rather than sons and daughters of God, and look at the examples of how Old Covenant saints behaved, the New Covenant saints allow themselves to be more like the Old Covenant saints than like Jesus, the Son of God.

# ARE YOU STUCK IN THE SPIRITUAL BIRTH CANAL?

How do we get stuck in the Spiritual Birth Canal? We get stuck when we have not had water immersion baptism or baptism of the Holy Spirit manifested by speaking in tongues. We are yet to enter the Spiritual Birth Canal if we have not yet manifested faith by believing in God, repenting of our sins and calling on Jesus to forgive us and be our Lord and Savior.

We may want the power of a resurrected life, but we may not believe we need to have water immersion baptism. Water immersion for spiritual purposes was not started by John the Baptist. The Mikvah (Jewish ritual water immersion) was a spiritual act done by the Jewish people for thousands of years and continues to this day. Water immersion baptism by Christians is a sign of repentance of sins for the remission of sins and the start of a new spiritual life in Christ. The scriptures state clearly, "Be baptized."

## Acts 1:5 (KJV)
⁵ For John truly baptized with water; but ye shall be baptized with the Holy Ghost not many days hence.

## Luke 3:3 (KJV)
³ And he [John the Baptist] came into all the country about Jordan, preaching the baptism of repentance for the remission of sins;

## Acts 22:16 (KJV)
¹⁶ And now why tarriest thou? arise, and be baptized, and wash away thy sins, calling on the name of the Lord.

## Acts 2:38 (KJV)

38 Then Peter said unto them, <u>Repent, and be baptized</u> every one of you in the name of Jesus Christ <u>for the remission of sins</u>, and ye shall receive the gift of the Holy Ghost.

**Water immersion baptism represents by our actions that we have the faith that old things (our old man, our sin nature, and all of the sins we have committed) are gone and forgotten.**

## 2 Corinthians 5:17 (KJV)

17 Therefore <u>if any man *be* in Christ</u>, *he is* <u>a new creature</u>: <u>old things are passed away</u>; behold, <u>all things are become new.</u>

## Hebrews 10:16-17 (KJV)

16 This *is* the covenant that I will make with them after those days, saith the Lord, I will put my laws into their hearts, and in their minds will I write them;
17 And <u>their sins and iniquities will I remember no more.</u>

**Water immersion baptism represents our burial with Jesus into the spiritual death of our sin nature, our satanic spiritual DNA. Coming up out of the water represents our resurrection from spiritual death to new spiritual life, in Christ.**

## Romans 6:4 (KJV)

4 Therefore <u>we are buried with him by baptism into death</u>: that like as Christ was raised up from the dead by the glory of the Father, even so <u>we also should walk in newness of life.</u>

## Romans 6:6 (KJV)

6 Knowing this, that <u>our old man is crucified with *him*</u>, <u>that the body of sin might be destroyed</u>, that henceforth we should not serve sin.

## Colossians 2:12 (KJV)

<sup>12</sup> Buried with him in baptism, wherein also ye are risen with *him* through the faith of the operation of God, who hath raised him from the dead.

Even after Cornelius, his family, and his friends had received the gift of the Holy Spirit, Peter instructed the group to perform water immersion baptism.

## Acts 10:47 (KJV)

<sup>47</sup> Can any man forbid water, that these should not be baptized, which have received the Holy Ghost as well as we?

Jesus said that to enter into His Kingdom a man must be born of water and of the Spirit, the phrase "born of water" referring to water immersion baptism for the remission of sins. When we believe in God, repent of our sins, ask Jesus to save us (which He does), and get water immersion baptized, then we should know that surely we have been saved. If we do not believe in God, do not repent of our sins, do not ask Jesus to save us, and do not get water immersion baptized, then we should know for certain that we have chosen to be damned.

## John 3:5 (KJV)

<sup>5</sup> Jesus answered, Verily, verily, I say unto thee, Except a man be born of water and *of* the Spirit, he cannot enter into the kingdom of God.

## Mark 16:15-16 (KJV)

<sup>15</sup> And he said unto them, Go ye into all the world, and preach the gospel to every creature.
<sup>16</sup> He that believeth and is baptized shall be saved; but he that believeth not shall be damned.

We must not get confused with doctrinal arguments such as, "Are you saying that getting water immersion baptism gets you into Jesus' Kingdom?" Or "Are you saying that not getting water immersion baptism condemns you to Hell?" The answer to both these questions is, "No." What we do understand doctrinally is that Jesus provides us with a way of salvation which has multiple aspects resulting in a death-to-life spiritual transformation, and if we delete any aspect, our Christian lives will not be as strong as Jesus intended.

So if we have not had water immersion baptism, we seek it out. If we have been water immersion baptized but did not know what we were really doing when we did, we should now get water immersion baptized again, knowing what we are doing.

We may want the power of a spiritually resurrected life, but we may not believe in either the Baptism of the Holy Spirit or that the Baptism of the Holy Spirit is manifested by speaking in tongues. So we live our Christian lives as the apostles and disciples did after the first day of the Resurrection (John 20:19-22). But Jesus said that after the Baptism of the Holy Spirit, the power would come down. This power is distinct from the Holy Spirit. The Holy Spirit is God.

## Acts 10:38 (KJV)

[38] How God anointed Jesus of Nazareth with the Holy Ghost <u>and with power</u>: who went about doing good, and healing all that were oppressed of the devil; for God was with him.

## 1 Thessalonians 1:5 (KJV)

[5] For our <u>gospel came</u> not unto you <u>in word</u> only, but also <u>in power</u>, and <u>in the Holy Ghost</u>, and in much assurance; as ye know what manner of men we were among you for your sake.

## 1 Corinthians 2:4-5 (KJV)

[4] And <u>my speech and my preaching *was*</u> not with enticing words of man's wisdom, but <u>in demonstration of the Spirit and of power</u>:

<sup>5</sup> That your faith should not stand in the wisdom of men, but in the power of God.

Jesus never water immersion baptized anyone, unlike his disciples. This is because Jesus baptizes us with the Holy Spirit.

## John 4:1-2 (KJV)

<sup>1</sup> When therefore the Lord knew how the Pharisees had heard that Jesus made and baptized more disciples than John,
<sup>2</sup> (Though Jesus himself baptized not, but his disciples,)

## John 1:33 (KJV)

<sup>33</sup> And I [John the Baptist] knew him [Jesus] not: but he that sent me to baptize with water, the same said unto me, Upon whom thou shalt see the Spirit descending, and remaining on him, the same is he which baptizeth with the Holy Ghost.

We should not make getting baptized in the Holy Spirit complicated, because it is Jesus who baptizes us with the Holy Spirit. We do not need anyone else, although others may help us in being baptized in the Holy Spirit (see Acts 19:6). We simply ask Jesus to baptize us with the Holy Spirit, understanding that we have first made Him our Lord and Savior (as detailed above). We also should understand that the Holy Spirit will never override our will. If we decide to keep our mouths shut and not speak, then we know for a certainty that we will not speak in tongues or speak otherwise, since we are choosing not to speak. Jesus has promised that when we ask for the baptism of the Holy Spirit, the promise of the Father, the Holy Spirit will be given unto us in baptism. So we ask and then start speaking in tongues as the Holy Spirit gives us utterance.

## Luke 11:9-13 (KJV)

[9] And I say unto you, <u>Ask, and it shall be given you</u>; <u>seek, and ye shall find</u>; <u>knock, and it shall be opened unto you</u>.

[10] For <u>every one that asketh receiveth</u>; and <u>he that seeketh findeth</u>; and <u>to him that knocketh it shall be opened</u>.

[11] If a son shall ask bread of any of you that is a father, will he give him a stone? or if *he ask* a fish, will he for a fish give him a serpent?

[12] Or if he shall ask an egg, will he offer him a scorpion?

[13] If ye then, being evil, know how to give good gifts unto your children: <u>how much more shall *your* heavenly Father give the Holy Spirit to them that ask him</u>?

[Note: There are some individuals who may have difficulty at first speaking in Tongues. This may be due to a religious spirit who denies that Tongues exist today or who professes that Tongues are demonic. The answer to these lies is to repent of those beliefs. In this case, another believer could inform us that these beliefs are lies, have us repent, then cast the evil spirit out and so help us be baptized with the Holy Spirit by Jesus with the manifestation of speaking in Tongues.]

After Jesus baptizes us with the Holy Spirit, then power comes down on us from Jesus sitting at the right hand of God the Father, sitting on the seat of power.

## Acts 1:8 (KJV)

[8] But <u>ye shall receive power, after that the Holy Ghost is come upon you</u>: and ye shall be witnesses unto me both in Jerusalem, and in all Judaea, and in Samaria, and unto the uttermost part of the earth.

## Mark 14:62 (KJV)

[62] And <u>Jesus</u> said, I am: and ye shall see the Son of man <u>sitting on the right hand of power</u>, and coming in the clouds of heaven.

## Acts 2:32-33 (KJV)

[32] This <u>Jesus</u> hath God raised up, whereof we all are witnesses.
[33] Therefore <u>being by the right hand of God exalted</u>, and <u>having received of the Father the promise of the Holy Ghost</u>, <u>he hath shed forth this</u>, which ye now see and hear.

We may not feel any power, but by faith we believe we have it because Jesus said <u>we shall receive power</u> after the baptism of the Holy Spirit (Acts 1:8). We then manifest that power by living the resurrected life in Christ like a son/daughter of the Most High God.

If we are stuck in the Spiritual Birth Canal, then we should get unstuck by obeying scripture in regard to the way of salvation to be fully born again.

# STILL HAVING
# SIN PROBLEMS?

So we are fully out of the Spiritual Birth Canal, but we continue to have sin problems. To clarify, the sins that we are talking about here are gross sins (for example Galatians 5:19-21) and not, for example, missing the Holy Spirit's prompting to pray for someone which can be part of learning how to walk in the Spirit. After being born again, we should always be choosing not to sin. If we continue to sin when we do not want to sin, then we probably need spiritual deliverance from one or more evil spirits.

Let us recall the analogy (in the Spiritual Birth Canal chapter) of using dogs to represent spiritually unsaved sinners and cats to represent born-again believers, with dogs becoming cats when they are born again. A born-again believer still struggling with a certain sin is like a cat who no longer wants to chase cars but has a car-chasing spirit in it which impels it to chase cars. It is no longer natural for the cat (who used to be a dog) to chase cars. However, the cat could choose to chase a car. A born-again believer can choose to sin. However, it is no longer spiritually natural for a born-again believer to sin; something is wrong if a pattern of sin is present; an evil spirit is being forward and needs to be removed.

Satan is a fallen angel, and his main weapon is lying. He wants all Christians to believe the lie that they cannot have any evil spirits in them because they have the Holy Spirit in them. This is despite the fact that most people, <u>before being</u>

born again, did not sense or believe that they had evil spirits in them, only something called their sin nature which impelled them to sin when tempted. This is despite the fact that after being born again, many Christians continue to sin, regardless of their strong desire not to sin. This is a key sign of needing deliverance! We find ourselves struggling against a strong compulsion to commit a certain sin or certain sins.

Scripture tells us that before being born again, we can have as many as 6,000 evil spirits in us, as did the man from Gerasene, who had a legion of evil spirits (Luke 8:30; Mark 5:9). Though the Gerasene had 6,000 evil spirits, yet he went to meet Jesus and was able to come to Jesus and fall before Him and receive spiritual deliverance (Luke 8:29, 33, 35). Mary Magdalene had 7 evil spirits cast out of her by Jesus (Luke 8:2; Mark 16:9).

Paul the Apostle rebuked Peter the Apostle when religious Peter (Acts 10:14 "But Peter said, Not so, Lord; for I have never eaten any thing that is common or unclean") sinned by manifesting what might be called a religious spirit.

## Galatians 2:11-12 (KJV)
[11] But when Peter was come to Antioch, I withstood him to the face, because he was to be blamed.
[12] For before that certain came from James, he did eat with the Gentiles: but when they were come, he withdrew and separated himself, fearing them which were of the circumcision.

Experiential Christianity can be a spiritual pitfall for us. Experiential Christianity bases doctrine on what I as a Christian believe myself to have experienced instead of basing my doctrine on God's Word. If a born-again believer discerns that I, a Christian, have one or more evil spirits and need spiritual deliverance, and I have no sense that evil spirits are in me (my spiritual experience), but I know that as a Christian

I have the Holy Spirit in me (which I may or may not feel or experience), then I profess (my Christian Doctrine) that Christians cannot have evil spirits after they are born again, but now can only have, in the spiritual realm, the Holy Spirit.

If this were the truth, then after being born again, Christians would never sin. If this were the truth, then the scriptures which command us to put off the old man and put on the new man would be illogical and meaningless. Because of what we believe Jesus did for us, we are no longer servants of sin. We are now free to choose not to sin. Once born again, we can never be evil spirit (demon) possessed, because we belong to Jesus. However, it appears that because of our having free wills, we <u>can</u> <u>choose</u> to have the Holy Spirit forward spiritually, that is, we choose to walk in the Spirit and be led by the Holy Spirit, or we <u>can</u> <u>choose</u> to walk in the flesh with evil spirits forward spiritually, and be led by evil spirits. Being spiritually new creatures in Christ with the Holy Spirit indwelling us, we naturally walk in the Spirit without sin and thereby "keepeth ourselves."

## 1 John 5:18 (KJV)
[18] We know that whosoever is born of God sinneth not; but <u>he that is begotten of God keepeth himself</u>, and that wicked one toucheth him not.

## Galatians 5:16-18 (KJV)
[16] *This* I say then, <u>Walk in the Spirit, and ye shall not fulfil the lust of the flesh.</u>
[17] <u>For the flesh lusteth against the Spirit, and the Spirit against the flesh</u>: and these are contrary the one to the other: so that ye cannot do the things that ye would.
[18] But if ye be led of the Spirit, ye are not under the law.

Sometimes there appear to be legal aspects that allow evil spirits to still oppress us spiritually, albeit not spiritually forward, possibly from sins we have previously committed without repentance, or possibly from the sins of forefathers which have been passed down generationally. We should understand and believe that the evil spirits are no longer in the same position of spiritual authority in regard to controlling us since we have been set free from sin by Jesus and can always choose to have the Holy Spirit forward. If, on the other hand, we do not know and understand scripturally that we are no longer sinners, then the evil spirits convince us of a lie and torment us with condemnation, doubt, and fear for our salvation.

## Romans 6:6-7 (KJV)

[6] Knowing this, that <u>our old man is crucified with *him*, that the body of sin might be destroyed, that henceforth we should not serve sin.</u>
[7] <u>For he that is dead is freed from sin.</u>

## Galatians 5:1 (KJV)

[1] <u>Stand fast therefore in the liberty wherewith Christ hath made us free</u>, and be not entangled again with the yoke of bondage.

In these circumstances, evil spirits can be compelling forces that try to convince us to sin. We may not want to sin but find it very difficult not to do so. We can be tormented by one or more besetting sins. Simply put, experientially, once such an evil spirit is cast out, the born-again believer experiences spiritual freedom. With the absence of the evil spirit, the compulsion is gone, and the believer no longer commits the besetting sin and knows, therefore, that an evil spirit had been there but now is not.

There are two spirits that we typically experience with spiritually unsaved individuals. We can find ourselves dealing with people who behave spiritually normal; that is, their spirits are forward spiritually. Then there is a noticeable change, often seen in their eyes, and evil spirits become forward with spiritual behaviors such as lust, hatred, lying, or strife manifesting.

There are three spirits that a born-again believer can manifest: the Holy Spirit, their spirit, or evil spirits. Walking in the Spirit means that a believer chooses to have the Holy Spirit forward spiritually, mortifying the deeds of the flesh. However, a believer can let evil spirits be forward, choosing thus to sin.

After we are born again, we still have the same free will we had before we were born again. We are, therefore, commanded to be dead to sin. Born-again believers pick up their crosses daily by manifesting the faith that they have been baptized into Jesus' death on the cross, have been spiritually resurrected, and have the spiritual power to deny their old man and put on the new man.

## Romans 6:11-12 (KJV)
[11] Likewise reckon ye also yourselves to be dead indeed unto sin, but alive unto God through Jesus Christ our Lord.
[12] Let not sin therefore reign in your mortal body, that ye should obey it in the lusts thereof.

## Galatians 5:24 (KJV)
[24] And they that are Christ's have crucified the flesh with the affections and lusts.

## Romans 8:1 (KJV)
[1] *There is* therefore now no condemnation to them which are in Christ Jesus, who walk not after the flesh, but after the Spirit.

## Luke 9:23 (KJV)
[23] And he said to *them* all, If any *man* will come after me, let him deny himself, and take up his cross daily, and follow me.

There are only two spiritual DNA natures: 1) Holy Spirit, and 2) satanic. After being born again, we are in Jesus, and Jesus is in us. We each spiritually abide in Him <u>by our salvation</u>. Metaphorically speaking, a branch is either in the vine, receiving the sap of the vine and producing fruit, or a branch is not in the vine. A branch does not <u>try</u> to abide in the vine, because it <u>is</u> in the vine. Abiding in Jesus, we choose not to sin. Having been made partakers of God's divine nature, we open our eyes after a night's sleep, arise and naturally start "walking in the Spirit."

## 1 John 4:13 (KJV)
[13] Hereby know <u>we that we dwell in him, and he in us,</u> <u>because he hath given us of his Spirit.</u>

## John 15:4-5 (KJV)
[4] <u>Abide in me, and I in you.</u> As the branch cannot bear fruit of itself, except it abide in the vine; no more can ye, except ye abide in me.
[5] <u>I [Jesus] am the vine, ye *are* the branches</u>: <u>He that abideth in me, and I in him, the same bringeth forth much fruit</u>: for without me ye can do nothing.

## 1 John 3:6 (KJV)
[6] <u>Whosoever abideth in him sinneth not</u>: whosoever sinneth hath not seen him, neither known him.

## 2 Peter 1:4 (KJV)
[4] Whereby are given unto us exceeding great and precious promises: <u>that by these ye might be partakers of the divine nature</u>, having escaped the corruption that is in the world through lust.

New believers, the babes and children in Christ, are warned not to be deceived into thinking that once they are born again it is permissible to keep sinning.

## 1 John 3:7 (KJV)

[7] Little children, <u>let no man deceive you</u>: <u>he that doeth righteousness is righteous</u>, <u>even as he [Jesus] is righteous</u>.

Sinners, having satanic spiritual DNA, sin because their spiritual natures are from their spiritual DNA father, Satan. We are sin factories that manufacture sins. By His atoning death on the cross, Jesus not only covered all our sins with His blood but also destroyed our sin factories, the works of the devil.

## 1 John 3:8 (KJV)

[8] <u>He that committeth sin is of the devil</u>; for the devil sinneth from the beginning. <u>For this purpose the Son of God was manifested, that he might destroy the works of the devil</u>.

## Romans 6:6 (KJV)

[6] Knowing this, that <u>our old man is crucified with *him*, that the body of sin might be destroyed</u>, <u>that henceforth we should not serve sin</u>.

Born-again believers, having God the Father's spiritual DNA, the Holy Spirit, choose not to sin and, therefore, do not sin.

## 1 John 3:9 (KJV)

[9] <u>Whosoever is born of God doth not commit sin</u>; <u>for his seed remaineth in him</u>: <u>and he cannot sin</u>, <u>because he is born of God</u>.

In the verse above, "doth not commit sin" can also be translated as "refuses to practice sin" or "does not make a practice of sinning." "Cannot sin" can also be translated as "not able to continue sinning" or "cannot go on sinning."

Those who are born of God choose not to sin. Those who are born of Satan choose to sin.

## 1 John 3:10 (KJV)

[10] <u>In this the children of God are manifest</u>, <u>and the children of the devil</u>: <u>whosoever doeth not righteousness is not of God</u>, neither he that loveth not his brother.

After coming up out of the water at water immersion baptism, we should look to ourselves or others for possible spiritual deliverance from evil spirits. Since we have just repented of the sins which gave evil spirits the legal right to be present in our spiritual realm, and since Jesus has removed their spiritual, legal rights, we are able to have them cast out in Jesus' name by us or others through the Holy Spirit who casts out evil spirits with His finger. Having been born again, we are in Jesus' Kingdom. Whenever we sense we have an evil spirit within us, and consequently repent of sin, we can command the corresponding evil spirit associated with the sin to leave us in Jesus' name.

## Matthew 12:28 (KJV)

[28] But if <u>I cast out devils by the Spirit of God</u>, then <u>the kingdom of Go</u>d is come unto you.

## Luke 11:20 (KJV)

[20] But if <u>I with the finger of God cast out devils</u>, no doubt the kingdom of God is come upon you.

## Philippians 2:9 (KJV)

[9] Wherefore God also hath highly exalted him, and <u>given him a name which is above every name</u>:

The Holy Spirit may reveal Jesus as Lord and Savior to someone in whatever way He chooses. Therefore, a person may believe, repent of his/her sins, and receive baptism of the Holy Spirit, and then have water immersion baptism, or water immersion baptism followed by baptism of the Holy Spirit. The important aspect is to have both baptisms.

After we get born again, we are spiritual babes in Christ. We must drink in the Word of God, as babies drink in their mothers' milk, by reading the Bible and thinking about the revelations of the Word of God given to us by the Holy Spirit. We thereby deepen our personal relationship with God. If <u>we don't</u> drink in the Word of God, like babies who do not take in enough nourishment from their mothers' milk and who consequently are physically weak, our spiritual growth is diminished, and we are spiritually weak. However, if <u>we do</u> drink in the Word of God, we become strong and mature spiritually, can enjoy more profound understanding and insight into God and His mysteries (the meat of the Word), and are able to walk as spiritual adults in Christ. In the spiritual realm, we walk by faith, and faith comes from hearing the Word of God.

## 1 Peter 2:2 (KJV)
[2] As <u>newborn babes</u>, desire the sincere <u>milk of the word</u>, that <u>ye may grow</u> thereby:

## 1 Corinthians 3:2 (KJV)
[2] <u>I have fed you with milk, and not with meat</u>: for hitherto ye were not able *to bear it*, neither yet now are ye able.

## Hebrews 5:11-14 (KJV)
[11] Of whom we have many things to say, and hard to be uttered, seeing ye are dull of hearing.
[12] For when for the time ye ought to be teachers, ye have need that one teach you again which *be* the first principles of the oracles of God; and are become such as <u>have need of milk</u>, and <u>not of strong meat</u>.
[13] <u>For every one that useth milk</u> *is* unskilful in the word of righteousness: for he <u>is a babe</u>.
[14] But <u>strong meat belongeth to them that are of full age</u>, *even* those who by reason of use have their senses exercised to discern both good and evil.

## 2 Corinthians 5:7 (KJV)

[7] (For <u>we walk by faith</u>, not by sight:)

## Romans 10:17 (KJV)

[17] So then <u>faith *cometh* by hearing</u>, and hearing by <u>the word of God</u>.

Maturing as born-again believers - crawling, walking, and then running (the race: Hebrews 12:1) - should be the usual process as we grow stronger in the Word of God and have an ever-deepening relationship with God.

God forbid that we sin once we are born again (Romans 6:1-2), but if we do, we must truly repent of that sin and confess it to Jesus, asking Him for forgiveness. Jesus will then forgive us and cleanse us from all unrighteousness, and we are back in the Light with Him.

## 1 John 1:5-10 (KJV)

[5] This then is the message which we have heard of him, and declare unto you, that <u>God is light</u>, and <u>in him is no darkness at all</u>.

[6] If we say that we have fellowship with him, and walk in darkness, we lie, and do not the truth:

[7] But if we walk in the light, as he is in the light, we have fellowship one with another, and the blood of Jesus Christ his Son cleanseth us from all sin.

[8] If we say that we have no sin, we deceive ourselves, and the truth is not in us.

[9] <u>If we confess our sins, he is faithful and just to forgive us *our* sins, and to cleanse us from all unrighteousness</u>.

[10] If we say that we have not sinned, we make him a liar, and his word is not in us.

## 1 John 2:1-4 (KJV)

¹ My little children, <u>these things write I unto you, that ye sin not</u>. And if any man sin, we have an advocate with the Father, Jesus Christ the righteous:

² And <u>he is the propitiation for our sins</u>: and not for ours only, but also for *the sins of* the whole world.

³ And <u>hereby we do know that we know him, if we keep his commandments</u>.

⁴ <u>He that saith, I know him, and keepeth not his commandments, is a liar</u>, and the truth is not in him.

## 1 John 3:6-10 (KJV)

⁶ <u>Whosoever abideth in him sinneth not: whosoever sinneth hath not seen him, neither known him</u>.

⁷ Little children, let no man deceive you: he that doeth righteousness is righteous, even as he is righteous.

⁸ <u>He that committeth sin is of the devil</u>; for the devil sinneth from the beginning. For this purpose <u>the Son of God was manifested, that he might destroy the works of the devil</u>.

⁹ <u>Whosoever is born of God doth not commit sin; for his seed remaineth in him</u>: and <u>he cannot sin, because he is born of God</u>.

¹⁰ <u>In this the children of God are manifest, and the children of the devil</u>: whosoever doeth not righteousness is not of God, neither he that loveth not his brother.

The above scriptures sound like the difference between those <u>who are not</u> born again and those <u>who are</u>. If, before we are saved, we say that we have not sinned, then we are liars. For the unsaved, they need to know that they have an advocate with the Father, Jesus, and that Jesus is the propitiation for their sins. If we are unsaved and confess our sins to Jesus, then He is faithful and just to forgive us our sins and cleanse us from all unrighteousness. We get born again. We then have fellowship with God. We know God and do not sin; we keep His commandments. If we are unsaved, then we do not know God, we sin and do not keep His commandments. Those who are saved are born of God and His seed, the Holy Spirit, is in them forever. Therefore they do not sin, because they continually choose not to sin, condemning sin in the flesh, like Jesus. Our not sinning is the manifestation that, indeed, we are sons and daughters of God and no longer children of wrath.

We must have the faith not to sin. The faith not to sin comes when we have heard the Word of God (which creates in us faith) regarding the scriptures and teaching which have been discussed in this book, and we fully believe His Word: we are new creatures in Christ who indeed can choose not to sin which are our new spiritual natures.

Our state of being, before we are born again, is one of sin. To use the above scriptures as a justification that it is normal or typical for us as Christians to continue to sin after being born again is simply the wrong interpretation. God specifically says in Romans 6:1-2 "…Shall we continue in sin, … God forbid. …" and Romans 6:15 "… shall we sin, … God forbid." We only use the 1 John scriptures to justify our sinning in order to reconcile the conflict between believing that we are saved but continuing to behave as if we have not been saved. If we are struggling not to sin, then we need spiritual deliverance. We are called to always choose not to sin with the ability to do so with our "resurrected life power."

## 2 Timothy 2:19 (KJV)
[19] Nevertheless the foundation of God standeth sure, having this seal, The Lord knoweth them that are his. And, Let every one that nameth the name of Christ depart from iniquity.

## 1 Corinthians 10:13 (KJV)
[13] There hath no temptation taken you but such as is common to man: but God *is* faithful, who will not suffer you to be tempted

above that ye are able; but will with the temptation also make a way to escape, that ye may be able to bear *it*.

## Hebrews 10:26-27 (KJV)

[26] For if we sin wilfully after that we have received the knowledge of the truth, there remaineth no more sacrifice for sins,

[27] But a certain fearful looking for of judgment and fiery indignation, which shall devour the adversaries.

We can choose to sin after being born again, but we should all have that an almost nonexistent mishap. Because God's Word tells us what Jesus has done for us, we have believed and received Jesus, who gave us the power to become sons and daughters of God (John 1:12).

# THE CHRISTIAN LIFE IS SUPERNATURAL

The conceptualization of the sin nature as spiritual DNA is a spiritual revelation that helps us to know Jesus better and to know our identity in Christ more completely. It is not intended to be used as an absolute doctrine but rather as a useful tool to have a more intimate relationship with God and to walk supernaturally with the Holy Spirit guiding us.

To walk in the Spirit and to live a supernatural life, New Covenant saints must understand and believe that they are new creatures in Christ, are spiritually resurrected from their old, dead, sinful, spiritual lives, and have become spiritually alive as sons and daughters of a Holy Father. The life of faith is the supernatural life that begins when the Word of God proceeding from God's mouth creates faith. This happens when New Covenant saints hear and receive His Word, and by faith, live their lives as those who are justified in Christ Jesus. This is how the justified have life and how they are to live – by faith.

## Matthew 4:4 (KJV)
⁴ But he answered and said, It is written, Man shall not **live** by bread alone, but by **every word** that proceedeth **out of the mouth of God**.

## Romans 10:17 (KJV)
¹⁷ So then **faith** *cometh* by hearing, and hearing by **the word of God**.

## Habakkuk 2:4 (KJV)

[4] Behold, his soul *which* is lifted up is not upright in him: but **the just** shall **live** by his **faith**.

Thus, we stay alive not only by eating food, but by every Word coming out of God's mouth. God's Words create faith. We who are born again and justified by Christ live moment by moment by faith walking in the Holy Spirit.

## Galatians 2:20 (KJV)

[20] I am crucified with Christ: nevertheless <u>I live</u>; yet not I, but Christ liveth in me: and <u>the life which I now live in the flesh I live by the faith</u> of the Son of God, who loved me, and gave himself for me.

We are to believe what Jesus said about those who believe in Him.

## John 14:12 (KJV)

[12] Verily, verily, I say unto you, <u>He that believeth on me</u>, <u>the works that I do shall he do also</u>; <u>and greater *works* than these shall he do</u>; because I go unto my Father.

The works Jesus mentions are the supernatural works that showed that God the Father was in Him.

## John 14:9-11 (KJV)

[9] Jesus saith unto him, Have I been so long time with you, and yet hast thou not known me, Philip? <u>he that hath seen me hath seen the Father</u>; and how sayest thou *then*, Shew us the Father?
[10] Believest thou not that <u>I am in the Father, and the Father in me</u>? the words that I speak unto you I speak not of myself: but the Father that dwelleth in me, he doeth the works.
[11] <u>Believe me that I *am* in the Father, and the Father in me</u>: or else <u>believe me for the very works' sake</u>.

New Covenant saints are to do supernatural works that show that God is their Father, that the Holy Spirit is in them, and that it is Jesus who does the works, just as he did in the Gospels through healing, raising the dead, casting out demons, changing water into wine, quieting the waves, and countless other miracles.

## Mark 16:15-18 (KJV)

[15] And he said unto them, Go ye into all the world, and preach the gospel to every creature.

[16] He that believeth and is baptized shall be saved; but he that believeth not shall be damned.

[17] And <u>these signs shall follow them that believe; In my name shall they cast out devils; they shall speak with new tongues;</u>

[18] <u>They shall take up serpents; and if they drink any deadly thing, it shall not hurt them; they shall lay hands on the sick, and they shall recover.</u>

## Galatians 3:1-5 (KJV)

[1] O foolish Galatians, who hath bewitched you, that ye should not obey the truth, before whose eyes Jesus Christ hath been evidently set forth, crucified among you?

[2] This only would I learn of you, <u>Received ye the Spirit</u> by the works of the law, or <u>by the hearing of faith</u>?

[3] Are ye so foolish? having begun in the Spirit, are ye now made perfect by the flesh?

[4] Have ye suffered so many things in vain? if *it be* yet in vain.

[5] He therefore that ministereth to you the Spirit, and <u>worketh miracles among you,</u> *doeth he it* by the works of the law, or <u>by the hearing of faith</u>?

The Holy Spirit is God. The Holy Spirit is in New Covenant believers, and He is the same yesterday, today, and tomorrow. The Christian life is Supernatural.

## 1 Corinthians 12:28 (KJV)

[28]And <u>God hath set some in the church</u>, first apostles, secondarily prophets, thirdly teachers, after that miracles, then gifts of healings, helps, governments, diversities of tongues.

Both Paul (2 Corinthians 12:1-4) and John (Revelation 4:1-2) went to Heaven and spoke about it.

Stephen (Acts 7:55) looked into Heaven and saw Jesus standing on the right hand of God the Father.

An angel (Acts 5:18-20) of the Lord opened prison doors, released the captive apostles, and instructed them what to do.

Philip (Acts 8:27, 39-40) was caught away from the Ethiopian eunuch by the Spirit of the Lord and was found at Azotus.

Peter (Acts 9:37, 40-41) raised Lydda from the dead.

Agabus (Acts 11:27-28) prophesied that there would be a great scarcity throughout all the world which happened during the Roman rule of Claudius Caesar.

Paul (Acts 14:8-10) healed a man at Lystra, impotent in his feet and crippled from his mother's womb. The man had never walked, but after the man was healed, he not only walked but leapt for joy.

When Paul (Acts 16:16-18) was in the city of Thyatira, he cast out of a woman a spirit of divination. Later (Acts 16:25-26), Paul prayed and sang praises unto God, and an earthquake occurred. All of the prison doors were opened, and all of the prisoners' bands were loosed.

In Ephesus, Paul (Acts 19:5-6), after certain disciples had been water immersion baptized in the name of the Lord Jesus, laid his hands upon them. They were then baptized with the Holy Spirit, after which the disciples spoke with tongues and prophesied.

In Caesarea, the four daughters (Acts 21:9) of Philip the evangelist prophesied.

As born-again believers, New Covenant saints are to live their Christian lives manifesting resurrection power, because Christ lives in them. By so doing, they will do works that glorify God their Father.

## John 11:25 (KJV)
²⁵ Jesus said unto her, <u>I am the resurrection</u>, and the life: he that believeth in me, though he were dead, yet shall he live:

## Philippians 3:10 (KJV)
¹⁰ That I may know him, <u>and the power of his resurrection</u>, and the fellowship of his sufferings, being made conformable unto his death;

## Ephesians 1:17-23 (KJV)
¹⁷ <u>That</u> the <u>God</u> of our Lord Jesus Christ, the Father of glory, <u>may give unto you the spirit of wisdom and revelation in the knowledge of him</u>:
¹⁸ The eyes of your understanding being enlightened; <u>that ye may know what is the hope of his calling, and what the riches of the glory of his inheritance in the saints,</u>
¹⁹ And <u>what</u> *is* <u>the exceeding greatness of his power to us-ward who believe, according to the working of his mighty power,</u>
²⁰ <u>Which he wrought in Christ, when he raised him from the dead</u>, and set *him* at his own right hand in the heavenly *places*,
²¹ Far above all principality, and power, and might, and dominion, and every name that is named, not only in this world, but also in that which is to come:
²² And hath put all *things* under his feet, and <u>gave him *to be* the head over all *things* to the church,</u>
²³ <u>Which is his body, the fulness of him that filleth all in all.</u>

Jesus' salvation is a radical, supernatural, good, spiritual transformation. Sinners are changed to New Covenant saints and reborn from sons and daughters of Satan to sons and daughters of God. Salvation does not simply change bad sinners into good sinners. It does not simply make sons and daughters of Satan into distant relatives of Satan.

Jesus' salvations change us from possessed by and possessing evil spirits (our sin natures) to being filled by the Holy Spirit who casts evil spirits out of us. We are translated out of Satan's kingdom into Jesus' Kingdom. No longer are we in darkness and deceived, but we are in the light and know the Truth.

Before being saved by Jesus, we think we are not so bad, but we are greatly deceived. Yes, we who seemed so good! We are altogether bad. Before Jesus' salvation, we are capable of committing the very worst sins, and would do so if given enough reason. To confirm this, all we have to do is look at the people in this world who have done and are doing the most horrible and heinous acts of evil. In the end, there are no "nice guy" sinners. There are none righteous, no, not one (Romans 3:10).

"Do not be deceived!" means that we are deceived before we are saved by Jesus (Galatians 6:7; Romans 7:11). We are in darkness and do not know the Truth of Jesus (John 14:6). We are headed to eternal death in Hell. By salvation in Jesus, we are changed to sons and daughters of God on our way to eternal life in Heaven.

Jesus triumphed over Satan. This is why we are more than conquerors; Jesus destroyed the works of the devil.

## Hebrews 2:14 (KJV)

[14] Forasmuch then as the children are partakers of flesh and blood, he also himself likewise took part of the same; that

through death he might destroy him that had the power of death, that is, the devil;

## Romans 8:37 (KJV)
[37] Nay, in all these things we are more than conquerors through him that loved us.

## 1 John 3:8 (KJV)
[8] He that committeth sin is of the devil; for the devil sinneth from the beginning. For this purpose the Son of God was manifested, that he might destroy the works of the devil.

One of the most important aspects of the Christian Supernatural Life is talking with God – Father, Son, and Holy Spirit. He talks to us, so we talk to Him. Sometimes, we pray in the natural. Sometimes we pray in the Spirit (praying in tongues). God loves us absolutely, and we love Him because He first loved us.

## 1 John 4:19 (KJV)
[19] We love him, because he first loved us.

It is not to the full glory of God when New Covenant saints have no supernatural power but only have teachings to offer to the unsaved as well as saved.

## 1 Corinthians 2:4-5 (KJV)
[4] And my speech and my preaching *was* not with enticing words of man's wisdom, but in demonstration of the Spirit and of power:
[5] That your faith should not stand in the wisdom of men, but in the power of God.

Teachings can be helpful, since they can be inspired by the Word of God and communicate the Gospel leading to faith and salvation. However, the lives of born again, resurrected, believers are supernatural at their foundations.

The Christian life is not an intellectual philosophy which believers must study, learn, and try out in hopes of an increasingly moral life. New Covenant saints are to introduce non-believers to the supernatural living God, Jesus, who has the answers to all of their questions and the provisions for all of their needs.

The advantage of using the spiritual DNA analogy for Christians is a fuller understanding of Jesus' salvation and an identity that is fully born again, both leading to a life lived in resurrection power. Furthermore, it helps believers to explain to unsaved people that we are all born with sin natures (spiritual DNAs from Satan) and that doing good things will not change our eternal destination, the Lake of Fire. Whether the unsaved is a "nice guy" sinner or a "wicked" sinner is not the critical issue. It is their sinner status that needs to be changed. The only way is through Jesus' great salvation. Only by choosing to be born again do we escape the penalty for all our sins; we cause, as it were, a crop failure and do not get the harvest we deserve!

## 2 Corinthians 6:2 (KJV)
[2] (For he saith, I have heard thee in a time accepted, and in the day of salvation have I succoured thee: behold, now _is_ the accepted time; behold, now _is_ the day of salvation.)

## Romans 10:13 (KJV)
[13] For whosoever shall call upon the name of the Lord shall be saved.

If you are not born again, then you must not wait a moment more before you choose to get saved! For God truly loves you regardless of what you may or may not have done in your life. His Son's blood can cover even the most wicked sin when you repent of it. God the Father has spiritually put into you a wonderful spiritual destiny in Him, which you can start to fulfill once you become His child and become free from Satan's power. Do it now. Call on the Lord Jesus. He is eager for you to choose Eternal Life. Choose Him now.

Made in the USA
Middletown, DE
24 April 2023